BACK TO THE ROOTS

Richard Mabey is one of the most influential conservationists today; also a successful natural history writer, he is concerned that the natural world should not become the preserve of the scientist. He is the author of *The Common Ground*, *The Flowering of Britain*, and the bestselling *Food for Free* and *The Unofficial Countryside*. He is also a regular broadcaster, reviewer, critic and columnist.

Richard Mabey is currently working on a biography of Gilbert White with the assistance of a Leverhulme Trust award.

Francesca Greenoak worked as an editor at Penguin Books before becoming a full-time writer and freelance editor in 1974. She has a special interest in our attitudes to wildlife, past and present, and her published books include *All the Birds of the Air* (1979) and *Forgotten Fruits* (1983). Francesca Greenoak has two children.

Richard and Francesca are old friends and close neighbours in the Chilterns. Many of the ideas in this book are the product of a decade of discussions, shared gardening experiments, plant swopping and, more recently, working to restore a nearby wood for the use of the local community.

Richard Mabey
and Francesca Greenoak

BACK TO THE ROOTS

A CHANNEL FOUR BOOK

An Arena Book

Published by
Arrow Books Limited
17–21 Conway Street, London W1P 6JD

An imprint of the Hutchinson Publishing Group

London Melbourne Sydney Auckland
Johannesburg and agencies throughout
the world

First published 1983
© Richard Mabey and Francesca Greenoak 1983

Set in Linotron Plantin by
Rowland Phototypesetting Ltd
Bury St Edmunds, Suffolk

Printed in Great Britain by
The Anchor Press Ltd,
and bound by William Brendon & Son Ltd,
both of Tiptree, Essex

ISBN 0 09 931450 9

Contents

Acknowledgements

We would like to thank the following for their help:

Bill Baker; Harry Baker of the Royal Horticultural Society; Peter Beales; Jack Boyce; Humphrey Brooke; Frank Carter; Richard Cawthorne; John Chambers; Deacons Nurseries; Lawrence Hills and Patrick Hughes of the Henry Doubleday Research Association; Philip House of Family Trees; David Horrobin of Efamol; Dr Stewart Johnson of the London Migraine Clinic; John Kilpatrick; Joy Larkcom; Jack Matthews; Patrick Matthews; Mary Mottram of Cottage Flowers Old and New; The National Fruit Trials; The National Vegetable Research Association at Willesbourne; Philip Oswald; Patrick Roper; David Smith; Muriel Smith; Anne Scott-James; John and Caroline Stevens of Suffolk Herbs; Ruth Thompson of Oak Cottage Herb Farm; I. S. Unwin Ltd; Terry Wells of the Institute of Terrestrial Ecology.

*An asterisk in the text denotes
names and addresses listed in the
individual directories for each section.

Introduction

At almost exactly the moment (4004 BC) that Bishop Ussher calculated Eden was created, a group of enterprising settlers down in Somerset were doing some ambitious landscape gardening of their own. Anyone with a boggy lawn will sympathize with their problem and be lost in admiration for their solution. Faced with the quaking wastes of the Somerset marshlands to negotiate, they built themselves a vast network of rustic walkways. They are still there, preserved by the peat: carefully grown and neatly cut poles of ash, elm, lime, oak, alder, hazel and holly, carpentered into efficient (and oddly attractive) hurdles.

We have scarcely looked back since. From Celtic tree worshippers, Old English fruit gourmets and Saxon herbalists, to Victorian rosarians, cottage garden revivalists and green pharmacists, the British have been famous for their long love affair (or is it an obsession?) with plants. It isn't that plants play a central part in our lives, as they do in countries where there is still a peasant economy; we haven't the right climate or a rich enough flora or sufficient distance from industry for that. What marks

Some seventeenth-century garden specialities: 'gilloflowers or pinkes'
and double daisies

out our relationship with what we might call 'domestic' plants is not so much dependence as a pervasive enthusiasm and ingenuity – regardless of circumstances. One of the most inventive bursts of creative plantcraft came about in the heart of the industrial north in the nineteenth century, when the newly created class of landless urban workers began developing varieties of everything from gillyflowers to gooseberries in their tiny backyards and windowboxes.

Since then, the world of plant-fancying has been rather overtaken by industrialized horticulture, and by the trend towards uniformity and convenience that has characterized every other avenue of social and economic life. But just as the worst insults of this development are coming to fruition, in simultaneous attacks upon our heritage of wild *and* cultivated plants (including making the sale of many illegal), a revival of the great tradition has begun. It has embraced not just a resurgence of interest in old varieties of plants, decorative and useful, but a translation of the practices, the *style*, of traditional plantcraft to modern needs.

This is a handbook for those caught up in this revival, whether as aficionados of antique lettuce varieties or proponents of the planting-out of arable weed seeds on motorway banks. It is principally a directory of ideas and information, but we hope that some of the attitudes that characterized the tradition (and its favourite plants) will show through. It was a tradition of ingenuity, of thriftiness in the use of land and plants (never grow for one purpose when you can grow for two), fun (gardening is one area where the British are hedonists), and above all, sociability. If in the light of this last feature this book appears blatantly selective and partisan, we can only plead that the great tradition was also one that delighted in idiosyncrasy.

HERBS

The strict botanical meaning of 'herb' is any non-woody flowering plant, though for most of its history the word has been used to describe plants, woody or otherwise, which were medicinally (or at least domestically) useful. Since virtually all plants were believed to be active in some way, 'Herbals' (see page 28) amounted to complete botanical catalogues, with notes about the plants' uses and 'virtues' attached.

OCTOR BOKANKY, THE STREET HERBALIST.

From Mayhew, London Labour, c. 1850.

Lost and Found– Redundant Herbs

Changing fashions mean that plants are forever disappearing from kitchens and gardens, and sometimes, more appallingly, right off the face of the earth. Luckier varieties pass into obscurity for a short while, and re-emerge in a new hybrid guise or a new role.

So it has been with herbs, pressed into service early, and often suffering early redundancy. Mistletoe, revered in prehistory as the supreme symbol of life and fertility, passed into the twentieth century as the centrepiece of a Christmas kissing custom and then suddenly had at least some of its supposedly magical powers over tumours vindicated. Soapwort, once a laundering herb, lingered on at the edges of gardens until it was accepted there for its casual good looks alone. Unexpected virtues have been discovered in plants such as evening primrose, and time has reduced the once virtuous alecost, motherwort and vervain to mere curiosities. As for the Anglo-Saxons' 'atterlothe' we may never even know what it was. . . .

Now plant medicines have been largely replaced by synthetics, the common, current meaning of herb is a plant used to flavour food without in itself being a food. (Herbal used as an adjective has acquired pervasive overtones of nostalgia and wholesomeness, and in advertising is apt to pop up before almost any product.)

The magazine *The Herbalist* has a useful general definition: 'Herbs – plants useful or beneficial to man or animals', and this is the one we will follow below.

The Herbalist
Bright bi-monthly (85p) on useful plants, with advice on growing, cooking, dyeing, etc, historical features on particular plants and gardens, and useful news and calendar pages.
9 Saffron Road, Histon,
Cambridge CB4 4LJ

Top Nine Herbs

The Anglo-Saxons had nine sacred herbs, chosen for what were believed to be a general wholesomeness and a wide-ranging strength against every kind of affliction from dog-bites to 'elf-shot'. They were: mugwort, plantain, watercress, chamomile, nettle, crab apple, chervil, fennel and the so far inscrutable 'atterlothe'. They were a very practical collection; common for the most part, and easy to cultivate.

We have chosen a modern top nine, respecting the tradition that the herbs should be non-toxic and easy to grow, but also taking note of the properties that are usually demanded of herbs today: e.g. that they should look decorative rather than just dowdily functional; be aromatic, useful in the kitchen and valuable to other birds and beasts, and that conventional and herbal medicine agree that they have some mild therapeutic value. NB: Chamomile and fennel are still in the chart after 900 years.

• Borage, *Borago officinalis*. An annual with pure azure-blue flowers. Tends to straggle a bit, so grow it through other plants for support, and to encourage it to reach for the light. Then enjoy the low sun filtering through the petals and the fine, translucent hairs on the stems.

The star-shaped flowers look just as appealing floating on top of a fruit cup or Pimms (as they come, or frozen inside an ice-cube). In warmer and more leisurely summers, Richard Jefferies reported, borage leaves used to 'float in the claret cup ladled out to thirsty travellers at the London railway station'. (*Nature Near London*, 1883.)

The leaves are cucumber-scented, good for salads when young; also mucilaginous and mildly soothing to inflamed throats if used in a warm infusion.

A good bee plant when in full flower.

Borage

- Chamomile, *Chamaemelum nobile*. Perennial, with white daisy-like flowers and feathery, apple-scented foliage. An infusion of the flowerheads is slightly sedative and useful for upset stomachs. It's also mildly anti-inflammatory when applied to the skin, and lightens the tone of fair hair.

  C. nobile Treneague is a prostrate, non-flowering variety which is used for making scented lawns. It grew first in the garden of Dorothy Sewart in Lower Treneague, Cornwall, after she had planted out a single cutting of normal chamomile (probably from the famous lawns at Buckingham Palace). But this was clearly some kind of sport, as its unusually vigorous spread was lateral, it showed no signs of flowering, and was strongly fragrant, especially after rain. Now propagated as the cultivar Treneague this single clone is the source of all the non-mown chamomile lawns in Britain.

Most of these herbs – and an increasing range of others – are available by post from the suppliers given in our directory section. But you may be able to find them available more cheaply from street markets, WI sales, fêtes. Look for curiosities, grow them on, and begin swopping – or selling your surpluses.

Chamomile lawns can be hard to establish, needing a great deal of clipping, weeding and protection during their early years. It may be more sensible (and more rewarding) to begin by planting up a small scented 'seat' on a level patch in a bank.

- Fennel, *Foeniculum vulgare*. A feathery-leaved perennial reaching 5 feet in height, and a fine plant for the back of a herbacous border. (Bronze leaved varieties are also widely available.) The aniseed-flavoured leaves and seeds are important in both European and Asian cooking, and are carminative. The yellow flowers

Fennel

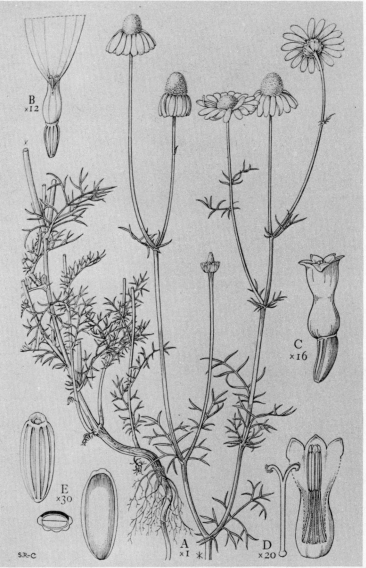

Wild chamomile, from Stella Ross-Craig,
Drawings of British Plants

(appearing in July) are very attractive to hoverflies.

- Garlics, *Allium* species. Spring-flowering bulbous plants with roundish (usually) flowerheads in various pale colours. *A. roseum* (pale pink), *A. moly* (yellow), *A. ursinum* (the white-flowered native known as ramsons) and *A. triquetrum* (the white bluebell or three-cornered leek) are excellent for naturalizing in grass or shady corners.

  A. schoenoprasum (chives) and *A. sativum* (common garlic) are the species traditionally used in cooking, but do try the decorative species as well (and don't forget the tree onion, *A. cepa*, page 80).

  All species are of proven value as gastro-intestinal antiseptics and for lowering blood fat levels.

- Lavenders, *Lavandula* species and varieties. Partially evergreen, shrubby herbs. Many varieties in cultivation (**Suffolk Herbs★** do a dozen) but some are temperamental and only half-hardy.

  Growing them against a wall, through old roses or with silver foliage shrubs helps protect them in winter as well as setting off their flowers well. Butterflies will visit them more in warm, sheltered spots, too.

  Flowers (attached to their stalks) conventionally used in wardrobes, especially in form of lavender bottles, and for making

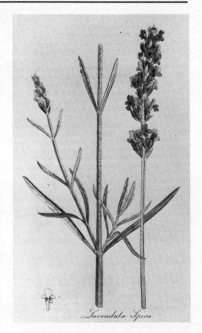

Lavandula Spica

Lavender, Lavandula Spica, *from Jane Loudon*, The Ladies' Flower Garden.

cooling lotions. But don't ignore them in cooking. Dried, and rubbed from the stalk, they are good in cakes and in spicy Provençal mixtures with hyssop, oregano and rosemary.

Infusions are slightly sedative, especially of the stomach and respiratory tract.

- Sweet cicely, *Myhrris odorata*. Tall perennial, dying back in winter. The finely cut lacy leaves make it a useful foliage plant for the border.

  The leaves are sweet, and can

be added to fruit dishes (useful for those on a sugar-free diet). The seeds, which resemble miniature gherkins, are aniseed-flavoured, and 400 years ago Gerard was recommending them: '. . . the seeds eaten as a sallad whilst they are still greene, with oyle and vinegar and pepper, exceed all other sallads by many degrees, both in pleasantnesse of taste, sweetnesse of smell and wholesomenesse for the cold and feeble stomacke.' They are often more than an inch long, so try them as a pre-meal nibble as well.

• Thyme, *Thymus* species. All are pleasant border and rockery plants, very attractive to butterflies and bees, and important culinary herbs. Their volatile oil, *thymol*, is mildly antiseptic, and an infusion of the leaves can be useful in throat or intestinal infections, or applied externally.

The Weald Herbary stocks 40 different thymes, including T. herba barona, *a creeping caraway scented species that is a good rock garden plant, and, for sentimental film buffs, the variety Annie Hall.*

• Woodruff, Galium odorata. Attractive spring-flowering perennial for shady borders. Has white, starry flowers. Leaves dry to the scent of new mown hay (due to the chemical *coumarin*, which in much larger doses is

used as an anti-coagulant in arterial disorders) and are included in fruit or wine cups.

• Mints, *Mentha* species and hybrids. One of the most versatile of all groups of herbs. Invaluable in cooking, attractive to insects if allowed to flower, and mildly carminative. If you don't object to their taking over the borders they

---

Herbs as Mirages

As an antidote to overfancifulness about savours and scents keep in mind Miles Kington's salutary reduction of all known herbs and spices to just ten varieties, including:

Fool's lemon mint. This is a rather attractive green plant with green leaves and green flowers which grows in other people's gardens. Take off a leaf, rub it between your fingers and smell it. It has absolutely no odour, but such is the power of wish-fulfilment that you will detect a strong fragrance of lemon, verbena, Roger et Gallet, chewing gum or whatever it is you wish to smell.

Frondwort. The basic English herb. It is an attractive green feathery plant and can be used in soups, stews, cakes and long hot baths. . . . Excellent in salads and on the covers of books about herbs.

The long straight dried pod. This, as the name suggests, looks like a mummified stick insect. It grows in the back of kitchen cupboards. It is excellent if dipped briefly in sweet sauces and puddings.

MS, London 1982.

THYMUS. Off.
Thymus vulgaris. Bot.
Der Thymian.
Ok. 1068.

An early variety of Mentha gentilis, *known as bushy red mint,*
Icones Plantarium, vol. 2

make very good ground cover plants, and have the advantage of blooming – in all manner of purple spikes and whorls – into that sometimes rather flowerless month of September.

Let them loose in a damp corner of a shrubbery, or keep them in check at the edge of a lawn, where they can be regularly mown. But don't put too much faith in the security of polythene bags, from which the roots will often break out in a free-range bed.

For smaller plots, try smaller and more restrained species, for instance the yellow-striped *M. gentilis* (often known as 'ginger' mint).

There are plenty of varieties to choose from. Most suppliers stock at least a dozen, and W. Sole's classic *Menthae Brittanicae* described twenty-four discrete varieties native or naturalized in Britain by 1798. Although it's hard to identify some of the types he describes, this is probably just another instance of *Mentha*'s tendency to throw up intriguing new hybrids. And Sole's vivid attempts to pin down the different scents of each variety are the best possible encouragement to keep looking for more. His corn mint 'has a strong fulsome mixed smell of mellow apples and gingerbread'. Water mint 'is exactly that of a ropey chimney in a wet summer, where wood fires have been kept in winter time', and his 'strong scented mint' has 'a very strong volatile smell of salt and amber, camphor and mint . . .' and is 'an honourable relic of our venerable Gothic ruins'.

For good modern descriptions, see Rosetta Clarkson's *The Golden Age of Herbalists*★

Herbs on tap

If you are growing herbs principally for use in the kitchen, there is much to be said for growing them indoors, in pots or small trays. It will encourage you to use them fresh, for a start, and is the best way of avoiding slugs and snails, etc, which can be especially troublesome in the case of basil, tarragon and parsley. But remember that most aromatic herbs like a warm position.

Herba Rara
some less usual herbs

- Alecost or costmary, *Chrysanthemum balsamita*, leaves, scented of mint and lemon, were dried and used as bookmarks.

- Burning bush, *Dictamnus albus*, the ultimate aromatic. Half-hardy in this country, but on a warm, still summer evening, the essential oils vaporizing from the leaves can be lit with a match.

- Camphor plant, *Balsamita major*, not true camphor, but similar smelling leaves used to deter moths. White, daisy flowers.

Iris florentina

- Elecampane, *Inula helenium*, tall, massive leaves, yellow sunflowers. Spicy-scented root used for sore throats.

- Fleur de Lys, *Iris florentina*, whose roots are dried to make orris, a pale-flowered hardy iris, available from **Ashfields*** and **Oak Cottage.***

- Three-coloured sage, *Salvia tricolor*, striking variety with green, yellow and purple striped leaves, beloved by Gerard and a feature of the Queen's Garden at Kew.

- Soapwort, *Saponaria officinalis*. Double variety has pleasantly muddled pink petals. Infusion of leaves makes natural detergent, whose use is described in *The Gardener's London* (Dawn MacLeod, 1972).

- Tutsan, *Hypericum androsaemum*, yellow-flowered shrub native in old woods and hedgebanks. Oval-shaped leaves dry to a warm, fruity smell not unlike Christmas cake, and were once used like alecost in the same way as bookmarks.

Good Scents

Along with their medical and culinary uses, their beauty and historical associations, the scent of herbs is one of their chief pleasures. The sweetest scented herbs should be planted along the main thoroughfare of your garden, to greet you as you return home, or as you make your trips to the washing line (or even to the dustbin). Place them so that you unavoidably tread them and brush them, and *don't* plant them too far away to reach and rub them between your fingers as you pass by.

Herbs underfoot: plant most of the forty or so species of thyme; mints, especially pennyroyal; chamomile, Treneague in particular. If you have difficulty getting them established *in* a path (or have the wrong kind of path) plant closely either side of it. Lovely near front doors.

Classical scents: lavender, cotton lavender, sweet marjoram, alecost, fennel, sweet cicely, pinks (a single packet of wild dianthus seed gives you more than you know what to do with), bergamot, lemon balm (grand for a dustbin screen), southernwood.

Acquired scents: these are ones to reach out for now and again: tansy, mugwort, lovage, sage, eau-de-Cologne mint.

Herbs for cats: cat-nip (catmint) makes them dopey with pleasure. (Also leave things about for them to cat-nap in such as a trug or basket).

Uses for scented plants

Mothbags: use wormwood, tansy, southernwood or santolina either tied in bunches or made into bags to deter moths.

Tussie mussies: a pungent miniature bouquet of sweet-smelling herbs: put in all your favourites, alternating form, colour and scent, binding them together with wool.

Sweet bags and scented sachets placed in clothes drawers or under your pillow keep their scent for a long time. They can be made from muslin, but they are best in a Liberty cotton lawn – you don't need much to make a few 3″ by 2″ bags. Lavender, many kinds of scented geraniums (perlargoniums) and rose petals are the usual bases, but mints, marjoram, rosemary and many others are equally success-ful.

Bath bags: cheesecloth or muslin, tied into a bag or sewn into shapes and stuffed with herbs such as lavenders, mints, lemon balm, bergamot, marjoram and rosemary – bog myrtle makes a bath to be remembered. Steeping the bag in boiling water for ten minutes or so and adding it to the bath is more effective than simply dropping it in the water or hanging it round the tap.

Herb pillows may be made entirely of herbs or with a mix of dried herbs and feathers. Make a tiny bag and stuff it with catmint for your cat.

Hair rinses: the standard recommendation is rosemary for dark hair and chamomile for fair, to condition and in the case of chamomile to lighten – but use a mix and enjoy the scent as much as the effect. Simply steep or simmer a few sprigs for up to half an hour in ½ pint of water. Use immediately.

Rosemary Verey's The Scented Garden★ *is a worthy successor to Eleanour Sinclair Rohde's 1931 classic of the same title (now out of print). Beautifully illustrated, it has excellent chapters on old roses, scented bulbous plants, twilight gardens and some highly imaginative ideas on 'heightened scents' – or how to enjoy fragrant plants without going down on your knees.*

Herb Gardens
'In a propre knot'

There are many intricate and beauti-ful designs for herbal knots, par-terres and other garden 'conceits' to be found in the old gardening books, but Thomas Hyll hit the nail on the head when he directed that his complicated 'propre knot' set with thyme or hyssop should be made 'for a Garden, where as is spare rowme enough'. Most of us simply don't have the space for something as elaborate as this. However, it is no bad thing to muse on the knots of the past and perhaps to apply some of the principles: the symmetry of the de-sign, for instance, some of the plant-ing ideas, the shapes of the beds.

Courtyards are good places to make herb gardens: a bare yard can be transformed, and rampant plants like mint can be restrained with minimum effort when planted in small separate beds.

Herb borders, cottage-garden style are very beguiling – watch you don't make them too wide, making the plants at the back out of reach. Helen Allingham's paintings are a useful guide to style and proportions.

Raised gardens, a medieval favourite and perfect for herbs – you don't have to stoop to sniff the leaves or pick your choice. A raised bank of herbs is also attractive.

Walls with bricks removed and filled with soil, for some specialized herbs, or a double wall with soil upon hardcore in between, can make small but useful herb spots.

Herb seats with brick sides and a surface of thyme or chamomile are a scented luxury.

Containers – sinks, buckets, tubs – fill them with herbs. A far cry from seventeenth-century knots but effective none the less. Don't forget they need more water than ground-grown plants. (Outside it is a good idea to grow your herbs where they are lit up by a light from a doorway or window at night-time, so that you can see what you're picking for late dinners.)

Public Herb Gardens

Before you decide finally on the shape and composition of your herb garden, sample the works of others in case there is a herb or planting idea you have overlooked.

Some famous herb gardens are: *Kew Gardens*; *Sissinghurst Castle*, Kent; *Abingdon Park*, Northampton; *Acorn Bank*, Temple Sowerby, Cumbria; *Hatfield House*, Hertfordshire; *Horsted Place Gardens*, near Uckfield, East Sussex; *Barton Manor*, Cowes, Isle of Wight; *Jephson Gardens*, Leamington Spa, Warwickshire (and see the directory for more).

In the Madrid Botanical Gardens, anyone asking for medicinal herbs between 11 a.m. and noon must be provided with them free of charge. The idea of providing a similar service in British botanical gardens – and indeed of creating special public physic gardens – was discussed during the closing years of the eighteenth century, when the College of Physicians was engaged in a fierce campaign against the more outlandish potions and practices (and prices) of the apothecaries.

Now's the moment to revive the idea. We already have extensive areas of public garden, often planted up purely for ornament with herbs and with that outrage against nature, the non-fruiting fruit tree. It would take only a little courage and imagination

(and certainly no more money) to make them productive as well, and encourage visitors to be active as consumers, learners and, eventually, contributors.

So why not have **COMMUNITY HERB GARDENS** featuring:

- well-labelled culinary and safe medicinal herbs;
- live presentations of unusual fruits and vegetables, old and new;
- fruit walks: cordoned and pleached for easy picking;
- seed and plant swop stalls;
- demonstrations of grafting, pruning and propagating.

Herbals

For thorough descriptions and assessments of herbals try to get hold of Eleanour Sinclair Rohde's *Old English Herbals*, or Agnes Arber's *Herbals.**

Wilfrid Blunt and Sandra Raphael's *The Illustrated Herbal** is a splendidly informative mixture of erudition and charm, and full of the most beautiful pictures.

Specialist libraries will sometimes let you handle the old herbals and sometimes they come up on the second-hand market. They are tremendously expensive. Occasionally there are reprints; at the time of publishing, a facsimile of Johnson's famous edition of Gerard's *Herball*

Ceres

Pomona

THEOPHRAST

DIOSCORIDES

THE
HERBALL
OR GENERALL
Historie of
Plantes.

Gathered by Iohn Gerarde
of London Master in
CHIRVRGERIE

Very much
Enlarged and Amended by
Thomas Johnson
Citizen and Apothecarye
of
LONDON

London Printed by
Adam Islip Ioice Norton
and Richard Whitakers
Anno 1633.

Io: Payne sculps:

(1633) is still available* though perhaps one should be warned by Raphael and Blunt: 'only those accustomed to let their Great Dane sleep on their bed should contemplate choosing the Mattiolus folio, or other such monsters as Johnson's Gerard or Parkinson's Herball, for a bedside book'. And there are always editions of Culpeper's *Herbal** about; read it for amusing glimpses of the wilder shores of herbal fantasy.

More readily available, and more manageable, are the few good modern works on herbs. Violet Stevenson's *Modern Herbal** (1974) is a model of its kind, practical, literate and quite outstanding beside the muddle of derivative bandwagon books which appeared in the 1970s. A reprint of Mrs Grieve's *Modern Herbal** (now not so modern, being printed first in 1931) is available, and though it's a shade indiscriminate in the information it offers, it is so packed with lore, quotations and recipes that it's still good value. Rosemary Hemphill's *Herbs for All Seasons** is first class on background and culinary uses. And, of course, for the most scholarly and stimulating account of the history and associations of herbs, Geoffrey Grigson's *An Englishman's Flora** is indispensable.

Dittander

The casualties of changing taste often cling on in the wild long after they have become obsolete. In the case of dittander, *Lepidium latifolium*, this was where it came from in the first place. Dittander's hot, spicy root was used as a condiment before the introduction of horseradish to this country in 1548. It is native in damp places in eastern England, especially by the sea, and naturalized elsewhere.

Although it is no longer available from suppliers, it can be grown quite easily from wild seed. Use it as horseradish.

Tab. 609.

Lepidium latifolium.

Pfefferkraut.

Ok. 1392.

Popular Remedies

Herbals and health food shops offer an increasingly bewildering range of herbal medicines, and it can be hard to sort out the useful from the unctuous. Plants have been elected to the herbal repertoire because of, e.g. the astrological associations of their flowering times, the resemblance of these seeds to bodily organs, and long histories of trial and error. From the latter tradition come many plant-based medicines (e.g. morphine, senna pods, quinine) used to relieve specific symptoms.

But herbalism *senso strictu* is not simply using 'plant medicine'. Three basic beliefs have run through it since the times of sympathetic magic:

1) that there are similarities between the physiologies of plants and people;
2) that 'whole plant' remedies are better and safer than derived and purified extracts or synthetic substitutes;
3) that the treatment of symptoms alone is not enough. Herbalists believe that treatment should be an advanced kind of nutrition, 'supporting the body's functions where these are seen to be deficient', as one practitioner put it.

Unfortunately, not one of these principles is always true, and though no one would disagree with point 3, diagnosis along such lines is so speculative and cures so protracted that it is all but impossible to show if herbal treatment had anything to do with the recovery.

None the less, there are developments in therapy which are tending to support at least the first and third principles and which may help close the gaps between conventional and herbal medicine. They are chiefly to do with exploiting the chemicals which plants use to regulate their own health. This has already happened with antibiotics, which are based on chemicals that plants use in exactly the same way as humans: to protect themselves from bacterial attack. Aspirin, which was first refined from plants, has recently been shown to act on them in ways that are analogous to its effects on the human body (it speeds up repair of damaged tissues, widens fluid transmission channels and fights infection).

In the body, aspirin acts through the recently discovered *prostaglandins* – hormones which appear to be involved in the second-by-second regulation of fundamental biochemical processes (e.g. the production and relief of pain and inflammation, maintaining the tone and sensitivity of tissue, skin, blood vessels). Prostaglandins act at the most basic cellular level, which is perhaps why there seem to be affinities between them and various active chemicals in plant cells.

Two old folk remedies, feverfew and evening primrose, have recently turned out to be exceptionally useful chemicals, if taken over periods long enough for them to intervene in metabolic processes at this basic level. More are bound to turn up in the future (some perhaps with anti-viral action: plants have been found to contain a kind of interferon). So do keep trying any herbal remedy you are sure is safe, and report any long-term effects, good or bad, to your doctor.

Feverfew
(Tanacetum parthenium)

Feverfew's ancient reputation as a headache and rheumatism remedy has been vindicated by work at the London Migraine Clinic. After a newspaper article suggested that chronic migraine sufferers should try chewing the leaves, so many patients at the clinic began self-medicating with them that Dr Stewart Johnson decided to start a long-term study of 250 takers (partly to make sure they weren't doing themselves any harm). The results were remarkable. After a leaf a day for three months, 70 per cent reported a significant reduction in the number or severity of their attacks. The active chemicals (called *sesquiterpinelactones*) have also been isolated. They appear to play some kind of protective role in the plant, and in humans act (probably via prostaglandins) as spasmolytics, stopping blood vessels going into spasm, which is believed to be the immediate 'cause' of migraine symptoms. The chemical may soon be iso-lated or synthesized, which will not please orthodox herbalists. In the meantime many sufferers continue to take the leaves regularly, and have devised all manner of ways of making them palatable, from feverfew sand-wiches, to pills made with the help of a blender, some icing sugar and a plaster mould.

Evening primrose

Evening primrose (*Oenothera* spe-cies) although well-naturalized in Britain, is a native of North America, and has no tradition of herbal use here. But North American Indians used the plant in the treatment of asthma and eczema, the significance of which only became clear when the chemical composition of its oily seeds was investigated. They are excep-tional in the plant world in contain-ing large quantities of gamma-linolenic acid (GLA), one of the essential fatty acids (EFAs) that are vital to the healthy functioning of the body. EFAs form part of the mem-branes that surround all the body's cells, and they play an important role – GLA especially – in the synthesis of prostaglandins (see above). If there is a serious GLA or EFA de-ficiency, typical twentieth-century chronic disorders such as thrombo-sis, arthritis and eczema start to appear.

Although human breast milk, sig-nificantly, is very rich in GLA, hard-ly any is present in a conventional diet. Under normal circumstances it's manufactured by the body from linoleic acid, which occurs in vegetable oil and offal and is common enough in the diet. The problem is that the conversion appears to be greatly inhibited by many items common in modern diet, notably saturated fats (from meat and dairy products) and alcohol. Taking GLA direct in the form of evening primrose oil is a way of by-passing this block in the conversion process, and clinical trials throughout Britain have produced remarkable improvements in patients with obesity, high-cholesterol levels and pre-menstrual tension. And the Indians' use of the plant for eczema and asthma has been vindicated by work with hyperactive children who had these disorders and who responded very positively to taking GLA in the form of evening primrose oil.

Evening primrose oil is, at present, expensive to buy. The large flowers ripen their seed pods successively over a long period, making it difficult to harvest them mechanically. An individual gardener could probably not grow a crop adequate to one person's requirements (one firm selling the oil suggests about a kilogram a year, which represents about 6 kgs of the tiny seeds). But a home-grown crop could be used as a diet supplement, with small quantities of the seed being crushed in a pestle and mixed with other foods.

Directory

Books

Arber, Agnes, *Herbals* (Cambridge University Press, 1938).

Blunt, Wilfrid and Raphael, Sandra, *The Illustrated Herbal* (Frances Lincoln/Weidenfeld and Nicholson, 1979).

Clarkson, Rosetta, *The Golden Age of Herbalists* (Dover, 1972).

Gerard, John, *The Herball* (facsimile of Johnson's edition of 1633 available from Dover Books).

Grieve, Mrs M., *A Modern Herbal* (Penguin, 1976).

Grigson, Geoffrey, *The Englishman's Flora* (Paladin, 1975).

Hemphill, Rosemary, *Herbs for All Seasons* (Penguin, 1975).

McEwan, Helen, *Seedgrowers' Guide to Herbs and Wild Flowers* (Suffolk Herbs,* 1982).

Rohde, Eleanour Sinclair, *The Old English Herbals* (Minerva Press, 1972).

Rohde, E. S., *A Garden of Herbs*, and *The Scented Garden*, both sometimes available second-hand.

Stevenson, Violet, *A Modern Herbal* (Octopus, 1974).

Verey, Rosemary, *The Scented Garden* (Michael Joseph, 1981).

Farms and suppliers of plants and seeds

(Many of these do a postal service)

Ashfields Herb Nursery, Hinstock, Market Drayton, Shropshire, tel: Sambrook 392.

Binstead Herbs, The Old Rectory, Binstead, Arundel, Sussex, tel: 0243 551277.

Candlesby Herbs, Cross Keys Cottage, Candlesby, Spilsby, Lincolnshire, tel: Scremby 211.

Chase Seeds Ltd, Benhall, Saxmundham, Suffolk, tel: 1728 2149.

Clive Essame, Oakmount, Honiton, Devon.

Down-to-Earth Seeds, Cade Horticultural Products, Streetfield Farm, Cade Street, Heathfield, E. Sussex, tel: 04352 3964.

Fernhill Centre, Fernhill, Sandyford, Co. Dublin, tel: 0001 989 158.

Flower Kabin, 18 Federation Street, Leicester.

N.B. It is always desirable to send a large s.a.e. when making enquiries or requesting a catalogue from any of the suppliers listed in this book.

The Forge Cottage Garden Herbs, Nr Woodbridge, Suffolk, tel: 072888 342.

Heches Herbs, St Peter in the Wood, Channel Islands, tel: 0481 63545.

Hereford Herbs, Ocle Pychard, Herefordshire, tel: 0432 78379.

Herbs from the Hoo, 46 Church Street, Bucken, Huntingdon, Cambridgeshire.

Herbs in Stock, White Hill, Stock, Essex.

Herbs & Spices, Garrick Farm, Andoversford, Gloucestershire, tel: 024 282535.

The Herb Centre, Thornby Hall, Nr Northampton, tel: 0604 740090.

The Herb Farm, Ivegill, Carlisle.

Highland Herbs, Newton of Petty, Dalcross, Inverness.

Hollington Nurseries Ltd, Woolton Hill, Newbury, Berkshire, tel: Highclere 253908.

Hullbrook House Herb Farm, Shamley Green, Guildford, Surrey, tel: 0483 893 666.

Iden Croft Nurseries & Herb Farm, Frittenden Road, Staplehurst, Kent, tel: 0580 891 432.

Lathbury Park Herb Gardens, Newport Pagnell, Buckinghamshire, tel: Newport Pagnell 610316.

Lomond Herb Nursery, Horsehill, Hoockwood, Horley, Surrey, tel: 0293 862318.

Manor House Herbs, Wadeford, Chard, Somerset, tel: 046 062213.

Netherfield Herbs, 37 Nether Street, Rougham, Suffolk, tel: 0359 70452.

Norfolk Lavender Ltd, Caley Mill, Heacham, Kings Lynn, Norfolk.

Oak Cottage Herb Farm, Nesscliffe, Shropshire, tel: Nesscliffe 262.

Old Rectory Herb Garden, Ightham, Nr Sevenoaks, Kent, tel: Borough Green 882608.

Oldfield Nurseries, Norton St Phillip, Bath.

Old Semeil Herb Garden, Strathdon, Aberdeenshire.

Poynzfield Nursery Garden, by Canon Bridge, Black Isle, Ross-shire.

R. V. Roger Ltd, The Nurseries, Pickering, N. Yorkshire, tel: 0751 72226.

The Springfield Garden Centre, Cranbrook Road, Hawkhurst, Kent, tel: Hawkhurst 3108.

Stoke Lacey Herb Farm, Bromyard, Hereford, tel: Burley Gate 232.

Sutton Manor Herb Farm, Sutton Manor, Sutton Scotney, Winchester, tel: 0962 76478.

Suffolk Herbs, Sawyers Farm, Little Cornard, Sudbury, Suffolk, tel: 0787 227247.

Thornham Herbs, The Walled Garden, Thornham Magna, Eye, Suffolk, tel: 037 983 510.

Tippell, Mrs J., 57 Ormesby Way, Kenton, Harrow, Middlesex, tel: 01 204 3663.

Tresare Herb Farm, Taman Bay, Looe, Cornwall.

Urban Herbs, 91 Clifton Road, Balsall Heath, Birmingham.

Valeswood Herb Farm, Little Ness,
Shropshire, tel: 0939 260376.
The Weald Herbary, Park Cottage,
Frittenden, Cranbrook, Kent, tel:
058 080.
Wells & Winter, Mere House, Nr
Maidstone, Kent, tel: 0622
812491.
Wilton Park Farm Market Garden,
Old Beaconsfield,
Buckinghamshire, tel:
Beaconsfield 3418.
Yorkshire Herbs, The Herb
Garden, Thunderbridge, Nr
Huddersfield, Yorkshire, tel:
Kirkburton 2993.

Societies

There are a number of societies and
centres which provide advice to herb
growers.

The Herb Society. 34 Boscobel
Place, London SW1. Open to anyone
with an interest in the history, development and continuing use of herbs.
At the society's headquarters there is
a library of modern books and research papers and a few valuable old
herbals. Publishes a rather scholarly
quarterly journal, *The Herbal Re-
view.*

**The British Herb Trade Associ-
ation**, Middleton Tyas, Richmond,
Yorks.

Our activities are concentrated on the
needs of industry as a whole: the
growers, the processors, the producers
and the suppliers to the industry.
Contact with the general public, apart
from the day to day business of our
members, is in the form of education and
maintenance of standards. Special
committees and advisory bodies are
established with responsibilities which
include standards and codes of practice,
scientific and medical subjects,
education and training.

Publishes a useful *Guide to the
Herb Gardens, Farms, Nurseries, and
Shops of England.*

Courses

Yorkshire Herbs,★ the largest
centre in the north of England. Week
and weekend courses, chiefly on the
growing and harvesting of herbs.

Herbs from the Hoo.★ Half or whole
day courses, under the direction of
Elizabeth Peplow. Covers herb
growing, cooking and marketing.
The walled gardens feature an outstanding collection of apple varieties.

Thornham Herbs.★ During the
summer Jill Davies takes weekend
courses in the surroundings of the
largest walled herb garden in the
country. The courses cover a broad
introduction to the landscaping and
cultivation of herb gardens, and the
collection and preservation of plants
for medicinal, culinary, domestic
and cosmetic purposes.

FLOWERS

There are more varieties of flowers which arguably could qualify as domestic than of any other category of cultivated plant. Even comparatively temperamental and exotic species like dahlias and petunias now seem thoroughly at home in the English garden.

But we're confining ourselves here to so-called 'cottage plants', which have the most interesting popular history and are currently amongst the most endangered of garden plants. As a group, they are easier to list than define and would include old roses, pinks, pansies and violas, lilies, geraniums, daisies, lavenders and primulas. It seems an odd list, but they do have certain qualities in common.

Botanically they are mostly hardy plants, bred (often by natural accident or amateur skills) from European wild species.

In terms of appearance their flowers tend to be pleasantly muddled rather than sharply symmetrical in shape, and in 'soft' rather than primary colours.

They also have a couple of what one might call 'social' values in common, in that they are long lived and easily propagated and distributed around a neighbourhood.

There is an obvious intrinsic appeal about plants with these features. But the choice of flowers grown in informal cottage gardens has also been influenced by a number of late nineteenth-century and early twentieth-century garden designers and taste setters:

- William Robinson, who waged war on the extravagance and artificiality of bedding plants, and in *The Wild Garden*★ and the *English Flower Garden*★ pioneered the idea of the naturalization and natural grouping of hardy perennial plants.

- Gertrude Jekyll, who pioneered new schemes of free-form planting and colour blending inside formal layouts. Read *Colour in the Flower Garden*★ and *Wood and Garden*.★

- E. A. Bowles, master plantsman and plant collector, whose objection to Miss Jekyll and her school was that their plants were selected 'merely as artistic furniture, chosen for colour only, like ribbons or embroidery silk'. Read *In my Garden in Spring*.★

- Margery Fish, who brought many of these strands together in a garden at East Lambrook Manor which combined foliage plants with old-fashioned favourites in a style that could be enjoyed on a small scale and at close quarters.

Not only was Mrs Fish the most generous of gardeners, but her garden was so thickly planted that when she dug up a plant for you, stray roots of surrounding plants came up with it, and you got a sort of lucky dip. I used to nurture these bits and pieces and they always grew. Some of these stray hairs grew into a colony of pink astrantias and others into a clump of white species of phlox; and there was the old-fashioned pansy, Irish Mollie, which Mrs Fish called Dirty Mollie, because it has a brown-and-yellow face in need of a wash.

Anne Scott-James, *Down to Earth*,
Allen Lane, 1981

Planting Cottage Gardens

The cottage garden is as much a matter of gardening style as plant content:

The planting of flowers in close masses is wholly modern. In the genuine old-fashioned cottage garden (now, alas, fast disappearing) we can still see the last phase of the old sparse planting. For instead of massing flowers of one kind and colour together in the approved modern fashion, the cottager likes a posy-like arrangement of his flowers, 'so that the place where they stand may resemble a peece of curious needlework or a peece of painting'. It is interesting to try and realize to what dim past this last phase of the old traditional sparse planting carries us.

Eleanour Sinclair Rohde,
Gardencraft in the Bible, 1927

Hoe down

Hoeing is effective but indiscriminate; hand-weeding is preferable in a cottage garden where tiny hybrid seedlings are very likely coming up along with the couch and ragwort. If you plant several species or varieties of one plant family, you are likely to find all kinds of hybrids appearing – insects not being purists on the subject of plant breeding. So take out the 'weeds' you recognize and leave in anything you do not. They may turn into something special only to your garden. Bill Baker, owner of a luxuriant cottage garden in Berkshire, abstains entirely from the hoe and follows this policy. He leaves his geranium species for the insects to work on and hand-pollinates his lilies – and has some very exciting offspring from both. Daisies, violas and primulas also respond to this kind of care (see later sections).

Plant barter

Gardening is by its very nature a generous pursuit: plants grow bigger and make seed and it is the easiest thing in the world to offer seeds and cuttings. Special associations too can come from plants which have been given by friends or remind you of a day out. Even gardeners of stately homes, botanic gardens and parks have been known to unbend and give away or swap plant material with those with an interest in and love for a particular kind of plant. And peering over a garden wall can elicit interesting talk about choice plants

Risen from the dead?

Cultivate the habit of nosing out lost and strayed garden plants. Good hunting grounds are derelict gardens (especially in the north of England and Western Ireland) and churchyards.

In *Old Carnations and Pinks* Reverend Oscar Moreton described how the old Stuart carnation, the Granaldo Gillyflower (a white variety, flaked and striped with purple), was put back into circulation after a Norwich lady spotted it amongst the flowers in a vase in a local churchyard, and was able to get hold of some cuttings.

Probably the best collection of antique pinks is that marketed by **Ramparts**★ nursery from Colchester, who stock more than thirty old varieties, including Bats Double, Bridal Veil, Charles Musgrave and Fountains Abbey. Recently added – and named – is Gavin Brown, a variety donated to them in 1980, which couldn't be identified and was therefore, according to time-honoured custom, named after its donor.

Two old-fashioned pinks: Young's Double X (left) and Mr Edwards (right).

from its owner and seeds and cuttings exchanges can be arranged.

Evidence of long-term barter may be seen in the gardens along old suburban roads, corners of villages and small cut-off communities. Signs to recognize are similar splashes of colour, or an unusual plant, replicated in several nearby gardens.

Primulas

These have some claim to being the most natively rooted of all our garden plants. Most garden polyanthuses and primulas (alpines excepted) have our native primrose, cowslip or oxlip somewhere in their ancestry. Apart from being highly variable species in their own right (both orange and red cowslips are not that uncommon in the wild, for example) these will all hybridize madly with each other and with other species in the family. Once richly coloured foreign varieties had been introduced here (like the magenta *P. hirsuta* from the Alps) almost any kind of seedlings could spring up in a well-stocked garden. The distinguished floriculturalist, Charles M'Intosh, reported in *The Flower Garden* (1839) that a Mr Herbert had 'raised from the natural seed on one umbel of a highly manured red cowslip, a primrose, a cowslip, oxlips of the usual and other colours, a black polyanthus, a hose-in-hose cowslip and a natural primrose bearing its flowers on a polyanthus stalk. From the seed of that hose-in-hose

*Hose-in-hose cowslip (left) and hose-in-hose false oxlip (right),
from John Parkinson's* Paradisi in Sole, Paradisus Terrestris, *1629.*

cowslip I have since raised a hose-in-hose primrose.'

As far back as the mid-sixteenth century Gerard was writing of some of these bizarre natural sports. He knew of: doubles, including a double

white primrose; hose-in-hose – varieties in which a second complete flower grows through the centre of the first; jack-in-the-greens, in which the flowers are backed by a ruff of miniature primrose leaves.

He also described 'an amiable and pleasant kinde' found growing wild in a wood near Clapdale in Yorkshire:

it bringeth forth amongst the leaves a naked stalke of a grayish or overworne greenish colour: at the top whereof doth grow in the Winter time one floure and no more, like unto a single one of the field: but in the Sommer time it bringeth forth a soft russet huske or hose wherein are contained many small floures, sometimes foure or five, and oftentimes more, very thick thrust together, which maketh one entire floure, seeming to be one of the common double Primroses, whereas indeed it is one double floure made of a number of small single floures, never ceasing to bear floures, Winter nor Sommer.

Might it still be there?

For the full history of primrose cultivation (and of many other old-fashioned flowers) read Roy Gender's fascinating Collecting Antique Plants.★

A large range of old, double, jack-in-the-green and hose-in-hose primroses is stocked by **Mary Mottram, Cottage Garden Plants Old and New** *in Devon.*★

She also often has in stock a variety of cottage plants, including double lady's smocks, golden feverfew, violas, Iris graminea (the plum tart iris), white musk mallow, purple four-leaved clover and hen-and-chicken daisy.

*Primroses: double hose-in-hose and Jack-in-the-greens
by Mary McMurtrie, from* The Countryman.

Left to right: Double primroses, gold-laced polyanthus and the show auricula Conqueror of Europe. From Jane Loudon's The Ladies' Flower Garden of Ornamental Perennials, *1841.*

A page of primulas from Parkinson.

These are some of the famous old varieties of polyanthus and primula which can still be found occasionally in specialist catalogues:

Silver Annie – a 'laced' polyanthus, with double mulberry flowers edged with a thin rim of silver.

Beamish foam – a primrose with a polyanthus habit. Small, pink, star-like flowers splashed with pale yellow.

Raspberries and cream – a true polyanthus, raspberry red flowers edged with very pale yellow. Reputedly still frequent in Somerset.

Tawny port – very dwarf with very dark flowers and maroon green foliage. Irish origin.

Lady Dora – a hose-in-hose polyanthus, with heavily scented golden flowers.

Gally gaskin – a jack-in-the-green single primrose, with a swollen calyx as well as a ruff below the flowers.

Lost

One reason why losses amongst old-fashioned primulas appear to be greater than among any other group of garden flower may be the wrong kind of cultivation. Many find their way into quite inappropriate sites in rock gardens or the dry edges of herbaceous borders. This may be fine for pinks and herbs but not for primroses, which like the same kind of conditions in which their wild ancestors flourish: rich, damp soil, sunlit in spring and partially shaded in summer. Most varieties will benefit from being divided every three or four years, and the doubles from a little extra feeding.

One probable casualty is Barrowby Gem, which began as a wild primrose sport back in the 1920s.

A true primrose but of a deep butter colour, the petals slightly thicker with just a suggestion of being frilled and very fragrant. . . . It is free flowering, very striking outdoor and delightful for indoor decoration. The raiser, Mrs McColl, told me several years ago she noticed a seedling primrose in her garden of a very charming shade of soft yellow. She waited till by division she got about a dozen plants and then collected seed from them. Out of 200 seedlings from these plants only one produced flowers of the same soft yellow, but it was of an even deeper and better shade. This is the primrose now known in catalogues as Barrowby Gem.

Eleanour Sinclair Rohde,
The Scented Garden, 1943

Wanda hose – a hose-in-hose form of the popular purple-flowered *P. juliae* 'Wanda'.

Bon accords – a set of a dozen double primroses raised in Aberdeen at the beginning of the century. They are 'bunch' primroses with some flowers being carried on footstalks as in the native primrose, and others appearing from a polyanthus-like stem. B.A. Gem has rosy-red wavy petals. B.A. Blue has huge amethyst blue flowers.

Gerard's double white – a very old (and probably natural) sport of the native primrose, with paper-white flowers held on long single stalks.

Marie crousse – very double blooms of deep violet, edged with white.

Red paddy – an old Irish variety of double primrose, with rose red flowers edged with silver.

Rose du Barri – probably of Victorian origin and one of the most beautiful of all double primroses. Large, cabbagey, pure pink flowers. Now very rare.

. . . And Found

Barrowby Gem is now on the list of threatened plants prepared by the recently formed **Council for the Conservation of Plants and Gardens**.★ The council's objectives include identifying those garden plants which are now scarce and whose continued preservation is desirable and important; monitoring those gardens that have important collections, and where necessary establishing 'national collections' of different groups of cultivated plants to act as public exhibitions as well as gene banks; and to encourage by every means, from education to the distribution of plant material, the widest possible dispersal of such plants in ordinary British gardens.

But the story isn't wholly one of loss. Recently found is 'Sue Jervis' – a double primrose with soft shell-pink flowers discovered in the wild as another chance sport. Available from **Bressingham Gardens**.★

Violas

To most gardeners violas mean either bedding pansies or the various species of violet. But between these is the whole range of old-fashioned violettas and violas proper – graceful, colourful, and beautifully proportioned flowers, and with unexpectedly delicious fragrances. They were enormously popular during the nineteenth century. Mrs Siddons loved them. The eminent jailbird Leigh Hunt, imprisoned for insulting the Prince of Wales, grew them in his garden at the King's Bench. By 1823 Henry Phillips (of *The Flora Historica*) punned 'thoughts are not more numbrous than the varieties of this sportive little flower'. Yet today they rank as endangered plants.

It was precisely the wild pansy's natural tendency to be 'sportive' that set the early pansy and viola growers into action. The native annual heartsease, *Viola tricolor*, occurs in a huge range of varieties, some deep purple, some mauve and yellow, some marked with blue and various patternings of rays and 'eyes.'

Pansies

It was by selecting the biggest and most interesting of these that the first viola family cultivars were raised in Lady Bennett's garden at Walton-on-Thames by William Richardson. Major advances followed in the gardens of Lord Gambier at Iver in Bucks. Working with *V. tricolor* varieties from Holland (and probably some native mountain pansies – see below) his gardener William Thompson was able to encourage exciting new hybrids and chance seedlings to appear in the garden, including the first all-blue variety. Then followed the famous Beauty of Iver, with a broad 'face' of pure yellow completely encircled by an edge of sky

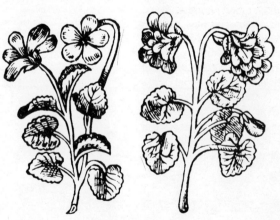

Single and double violets

VIOLA TRICOLOR. Off.
Viola tricolor. *Botan.*
Dreyfaltigkeitsblume.
Ok. 1375.

THE MOST FASHIONABLE
PERFUMES

Distilled from Fresh Flowers

BY

J. GIRAUD FILS,
GRASSE,

VENICE, and OLYMPIA.

Violettes de Grasse, 5/-, 2/6.

Violettes de Nice, 6/-, 4/6, 3/-.

Vanda, 4/6, 2/6.

Australian Bouquet, 3/6, 2/6.

Violettes d'Italie, 5/-, 3/6, 2/6.

White Lilac, 3/6, 2/6.

Lys du Japon, 3/6, 2/6.

Bouquet Fleurs de Grasse, 6/-, 4/6, 3/-.

H.M. Queen Victoria, when in Grasse, pronounced the Perfumes of M. Giraud to be "Exquisite."

Sachets of Artistic Design and Delicious Fragrance, from 6d. each.

Of all leading Chemists and Perfumers, or the London Agents,

BARCLAY & SONS, Ltd., 95, Farringdon Street.

Established upwards of a Century.

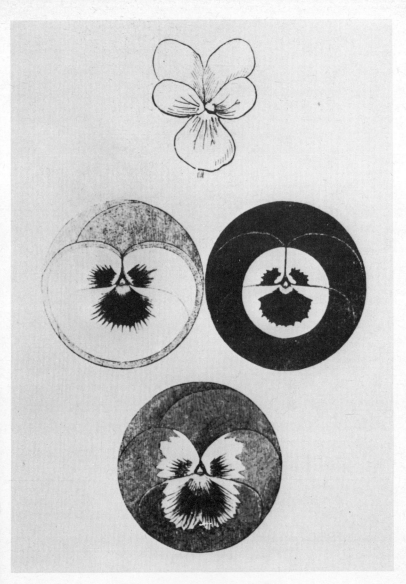

Perfectly proportioned and perfumed:
two ways violas were exploited by florists. The circular shape
was held to be the most desirable in competition.

Forms of the native mountain pansy,
Viola lutea.

blue, and Medora, the first of the now familiar 'blotched' pansies. These eventually led to the fancy pansies whose cultivation became a cult amongst the miners of north Staffordshire, and to modern bedding pansies.

The **National Pansy and Viola Society**★ now holds its annual general meeting in the autumn when cuttings are taken so that new members can have the benefit of these to form the basis of their own collections.

Violas

Meanwhile, the viola proper was being developed by James Grieve, of Dickson's nurseries of Edinburgh – and after whom the famous apple was named. His starting points were the pert, tufted species of northern European wild perennial pansies: principally *V. cornuta* (the horned viola from the Pyrenees) and various subspecies of our mountain pansy, *V. lutea*, which he collected from the Scottish hills (including the common yellow and mauve varieties), the larger, variegated and often bluish *V. amoena*, and the more prostrate, prolifically flowering seaside pansy, *V. curtisii*. From hybrids between these (and perhaps with *V. tricolor* based pansies) he obtained many intriguingly marked, compact and hardy violas, including Tory, Vanguard (now probably extinct) and in 1867 the pure yellow Bullion, still avail-

able from **Richard Cawthorne** (see below).★

But some modern authorities suspect that bumble bees did more of the crossing than gardeners, that the exact parentages of seedling varieties are impossible to determine, and more heretically still that there was little crossing *between* species, but a good deal of selection from amongst natural variations *within* each species.

Violettas

Finally there are the violettas, first raised by Dr Stuart of Chairnside, Berwickshire. They are similar to violas in being compact and clumpy, but lack rays in the centre of the flower, and have a strong vanilla scent.

The old named violas are generally very difficult to get hold of. Some nurseries will stock the most popular traditional variety, the silvery blue Maggie Mott, a few will sell the yellow and chocolate brown Jackanapes (raised by Gertrude Jekyll) or even the yellow-bronze Irish Mollie. Usually, however, you will have to find a generous viola gardener or go to a specialist cottage garden nursery (see page 67). The biggest and best selection appears in **Richard Cawthorne's**★ catalogue where there are over a hundred viola varieties and a good number of violettas, including the graceful White Swan; Primrose Dame; and the fine old silver-mauve variety Princess Mab.

In his notes Richard Cawthorne advises that violas and violettas prefer cool conditions as a whole – semi-shade if possible. Before planting dig in a liberal quantity of peat and bonemeal or organic matter and add a sprinkling of general fertilizer at planting time. Many varieties will bloom all the way from March until November if dead-headed.

Dead-heading helps ensure continuous flowering by stopping the setting of seed. If you do allow seed to form, you are quite likely to obtain some odd – and maybe attractive – hybrids or throwbacks from it (violas being highly variable and very prone to cross-breeding).

But do mark and label the named parents as well as encouraging new hybrids. So many of the old violas and violettas are under threat that it would be a shame to lose any. Richard Cawthorne will sell no less than three plants of any variety you order from him in the hope of giving them a better chance of survival. He concludes his catalogue with the motto:

The pansies, violas, and violettas of the world are not ours to dispose of as we please. We must make it our duty to hold them in trust, for other generations to follow.

Lost

Violas under threat: Dobbies Bronze: a fine bronze viola, blotched a darker mahogany, a very striking plant. Blue Cloud: a very old variety (recently rescued from Devon), pure white with blue margining, all the petals rayed.

. . . And found

Richard Cawthorne's own choice of the violas and violettas he has bred himself are:

Violas: Fiona – very hardy and highly scented with long-stemmed flowers; white ground, all petals slightly suffused with palest mauve.
Aspasia – large plant, top petals creamy white, lower petals deep yellow.

Etain – pale yellow, all petals margined with violet.
Letitia – very fine, pale red-purple with deep purple rays.
Lord Plunket – pure maroon-purple with yellow eye; large flower and long blooming.
Inverurie Beauty – very profuse bloomer, violet/mauve, rayed; the hardiest and most indestructible viola.

Violettas: Luna – palest of yellow flowers – highly scented.
Boy Blue – mid-blue, very hardy and long-lived.
Purity – excellent pure white, heavily scented, long-lived and very hardy.
Rebecca – deep flecks of violet on outer edges of cream-white slightly frilled flowers, heavy scent.

Wild flowers in the garden plot

There are many wild flowers which look very well in the garden, just so long as you don't desire neat, brilliant, homogeneous beds. Celandines, primroses, cowslips and oxlips, violets and valerian, foxgloves and poppies, agrimony and fragrant dame's violet . . . it's a rich and exciting range – but lest we get carried away with enthusiasm and strip the countryside for what may turn out to be a useless plunder, a few words on collecting British wild plants.

There are sixty-two species which are totally protected by law and for which it is an offence to remove any part of the plant. Since 1975 it has also been illegal to dig up any wild plant without permission from the owner or occupier of the land on which it grows. However, seed collection is permissible and, if done respectfully, even desirable. While a collector is unlikely ever to brush against the law (legally protected species are extremely rare), there may be species which are locally rare or endangered. *The British Red Data Book** lists several hundred species which are endangered or rare. The local recorder for the **BSBI*** (**Botanical Society of the British Isles**) will be able to advise on regional rarities and advise on species which should not be collected.

But most common species of plant produce more seed than will ever grow on, so taking some won't harm the existing population unless there are only a few plants, in which case it is probably best to leave them. Let the plant tell you when its seeds are ripe: wait until they come away or shake out readily. When you come to sow, remember the kind of situation in which you found your parent plants and find or create the nearest thing to it in your garden; there is no point in putting marsh marigolds or cuckoo flowers, marshland plants, in the driest part of a garden.

Traveller's Joy
Don't turn your nose up at our native clematis. Common though it is in woods and hedgerows on chalky soils, it is worth a second glance for its twining long-stemmed leaves, and of course for its feathery mist of plumed seed in late autumn and winter. William Robinson thought there was nothing better for 'quickly covering rough mounds or bowers'.

Nurseries are unlikely to stock it (so grow it from seed or cuttings) but Parkinson, who was strict on such matters, found a place for it in his Paradisus *and Gerard, whilst frankly admitting that it had no apparent medicinal value, loved it enough to give it the name that has stuck for 400 years.*

Daisies

Let some of your daisies out of the lawn and into the flowerbeds. 'The most eligible way is to plant them in rows by the side of walks' as an eighteenth-century clergyman-gardener rightly said. Pepper your pathways with native and double daisies and watch for the interesting variety of half-double and blended shade seedlings – and they'll do this in the poorest, stoniest soils.

Gardening books instruct you to dead-head to prevent 'inferior seedlings'. Instead, mix native daisies with miniature doubles Dresden China (pink); crimson Pompnette with small quilled petals; carmine Red Buttons and red Rob Roy and decide for yourself if your hybrids are inferior.

Try also the Hen and Chickens or 'childing' daisy (available from **Mary Mottram★**). This isn't so much elegant as curious: the central flower is a slightly scruffy double daisy, and round it smaller stems spoke outwards, each carrying a tiny daisy flower. As John Parkinson noted in 1629, the rest of the flower, leaves and roots are exactly as in other double daisies. It's too ragged and diminutive to make a show in the border but the flowers make an unconventional buttonhole.

Lost and Found

The following sports of native or naturalized British plants have all been taken into gardens, and still crop up in the wild from time to time:

Field poppies with pale pink petals, or white centres (cultivars known as Shirley poppies); double-flowered varieties of buttercup, marsh marigold, greater celandine, lady's smock and feverfew; white musk mallow and herb robert; purple-leaved plantains and yellow-flowered gladdons; copper beeches and weeping hollies; variegated-leaved heathers; the pale pink, prostrate variety of bloody cranesbill, *Geranium sanguineum* var *lancastriense*, which is probably an endemic variety, confined to dunes in north-west England.

All these varieties will normally grow true from seed.

But has anyone seen, either in the wild or in cultivation, the large flowered sky-blue wood anemone (*A. nemorosa*) that William Robinson praised in *The Wild Garden*?

Hen and chickens daisy by Mary McMurtrie from The Countryman.

Wildernesses in the garden

Easily overlooked but very beautiful are the flowers of our native grasses: the upswept head of crested dog's tail, the delicate bents, the bushy heads of meadow fox-tail, coloured orange or purple when the flowers are open, and sweet vernal grass with the original sweet hay scent when cut and drying. These unfortunately are the species most frequently left out of commercial grass mixtures. It is worth trying to collect some seed for yourself as it ripens in late summer, but if you have a large area to sow, it is now possible to get a good mix from certain suppliers (see directory).

The comparative ease with which wild flower species can be established in gardens (and in other artificial habitats) has meant a boom in the sale of wild flower seeds for sowing in anything from an untended corner of a suburban lawn to a whole motorway bank.

The leading merchants are **John Chambers*** (Kettering, Northants), **Suffolk Herbs*** (Sudbury, Suffolk), **Naturescape*** (Nottingham), and **Emorsgate Seeds*** (King's Lynn, Norfolk). All these suppliers attempt to use home-raised seeds from native British stock (and make clear in their catalogues where imported seeds have to be offered instead). They also supply mixes for building up different types of communities on different soils, and between them stock

most of the old cornfield weeds (e.g. cornflowers and corncockle) that not so long ago used to make our arable fields vivid with colour.

If you have no room for a garden specifically devoted to so-called weeds, try catch-cropping some in those gaps in the rose bed, or between rows of vegetables. Being opportunists by nature they thrive very well in these snatched spaces, and look good as well, back in their traditional niche between other crop-plants.

Flowerymeads

Creating attractive grasslands using native plant species is the title of a new guide published by the Nature Conservancy Council for all those interested in re-creating traditional grass swards full of colourful wild flowers. Modern farming has swept away most of the old meadowland in favour of more productive grass leys, but we now have the technology to produce something visually similar for landscape and amenity purposes – for public open spaces, for the verges of new roads, for orchards and private gardens.

The book provides a guide to the methods and techniques available for collecting, threshing and cleaning, storing and germinating seeds and propagating seedlings of native wild species, based on hard-won practical experience.

It recommends seed mixtures for two grass lengths on three different soil types. It also contains advice on

William Robinson's vision of a 'naturall wildnesse'.

A new tradition

Of the family *Geraniaceae* but really (like the so-called border and pot geraniums) pelargoniums, scent-leaved geraniums were something of a vogue during the nineteenth century. Since then, support has fallen away and many of the old varieties are extinct or at least unidentifiable. The lemony-scented ones are the most easily obtainable, particularly *P. graveolens* and the more muted *P. crispum* with small fan-shaped leaves which comes also in a variegated form: three or four of these grown in a spire make a splendid pot for the window. Less common are *P. fragrans* with a pine scent and *P. filicifolium* which has sticky fern-like leaves and a powerful sweet resin smell. Others smell of rose, lavender, orange, strawberry, violet and ginger, but these are more difficult to come by.

They were brought to England from the Cape by travellers and navigators early in the seventeenth century. They will thrive outside in pots during the summer months but need to be brought in for the winter, and are at their best on window sills or in alcoves. Place them, as the Victorians did, in places where you will brush against them frequently and where you can see the tiny flowers at eye level.

subsequent management of the sown areas.

The plant species recommended are all relatively common and widely distributed natives, so that their use will not cause scientific confusion by altering geographical distribution patterns. Re-created swards can never be a substitute for long-established meadows, examples of which must be conserved for future generations by traditional management; but they can compensate somewhat for the loss of colour suffered in the modern landscape.

Planting hints for native fritillaries

The snakeshead fritillary *Fritillaria meleagris*, is a lovely plant for a grassy bank (or a damp place in the lawn which can be left semi-wild and not mown until July), but one of the hardest to establish. Many suppliers sell fritillary bulbs, but people are often discouraged by poor success and high price. The little bulbs are very susceptible to rot; they are also very delicate and intolerant of bruising or prolonged exposure to air, so make sure you buy from a reputable supplier and handle them carefully when planting. The bulbs are crescent shaped; if you place them points down, or on their sides, at a depth of three to four inches packed about with a little sand, and try to get them in during the autumn you stand a better than average chance of enjoying these beautiful snake-headed flowers in May-time.

A bunch of Fritillaria species.
From The Ladies' Flower Garden of
Ornamental Bulbous Plants, *1841*.

Roses

The best-loved flowers in the world. The lure of their pure-scented, soft-petalled, sculptural blossoms has touched each generation even in the most inhospitable circumstances. Dean Hole saw roses joining the ranks of florists' favourites one early spring in the Black Country:

One cold slate-coloured morning towards the end of March, I received a note from a Nottingham mechanic, inviting me to assist in a judicial capacity at an exhibition of Roses, given by working men, which was to be held on Easter Monday. Not having at the time a Rose in my possession, although, to my shame be it spoken, I had ample room and appliances, it never occurred to me that the tiny glass houses, which I had seen so often on the hills near Nottingham, could be more honourably utilised or worthily occupied, and I threw down the letter on my first impulse as a hoax, and a very poor one.

On Easter Monday, in due course, upon a raw and gusty day, I went to Nottingham. Nor were my silly suspicions expelled until my hansom from the station stopped before the General Cathcart Inn, and the landlord met me, with a smile on his face and with a Senateur Vaisse in his coat, which glowed amid the gloom like the red light on a midnight train, and (in my eyes, at any rate) made

Lost

Native English wild roses have played important supporting roles in cultivation. The common field rose, *R. arvensis*, was developed into the rambling Ayrshire roses; the Burnet rose, *R. pimpinellifolia*, gave the early flowering hybrid spinosissimas. But little has ever been done with the deep red, velvet-flowered downy rose, *R. tomentosa*, and the only sweetbriar now generally available is the basic species, *R. rubiginosa* (the scientific name has now been changed from *R. eglanteria* to *R. rubiginosa*).

Not so long ago, however, there were several varieties of the sweetbriar. The 'large eglantine rose' or 'tree sweetbriar' was available well into this century. It is a natural sport and said to grow seven to eight feet in a single season.

Other varieties mentioned by the rose writer and expert H. C. Andrews are as follows:

R. eglanteria concava: flowers as well as leaves are concave, resembling little spoons. It flowers late in the summer and into autumn.

R. eglanteria pubescens: the only downy leaved eglantine, also known as Maiden's Blush sweetbriar. It begins to bloom in late July and continues for another two months.

R. eglanteria multiplex: Williams's sweetbriar, the double eglantine rose, best of all the fragrant leaved roses, known to Gerard in the late sixteenth century.

summer of that damp and dismal day.

'The Roses were ready: would I go upstairs?' And upstairs, accordingly, with my co-censor, a nurseryman and skilled Rosarian of the neighbourhood, I mounted, and entered one of those long narrow rooms in which market-ordinaries are wont to be held.

I have never seen better specimens of cut Roses, grown under glass, than those which were exhibited by these working men. Their Tea-Roses – Adam, Devoniensis, Madame Willermorz, and Souvenir d'un Ami especially – were shown in their most exquisite beauty; and, coming down to the present time, I do not hesitate to say that the best Maréchal Niel and the best Madame Margottin which I have yet seen, I saw this spring at Nottingham, in ginger-beer bottles! Of course, in an exhibition of this kind, with difficulties to oppose which few dare to encounter and very few overcome, these poor florists must include among their masterpieces many specimens of medium merit, and some failures. Among the latter I cannot forget a small and sickly exposition of Paul Ricaut, who, by some happy coincidence, which warmed my whole body with laughter, was appropriately placed in a large medicine-bottle, with a label, requesting that the wretched invalid might be well rubbed every night and morning. Poor Paul! a gentle touch would have sent him to *pot-pourri*!

Condensed from *A Book About Roses*, 1869.

R. eglanteria muscosa: mossy eglantine roses; Mossy sweetbriar or Mannings sweetbriar and Double Mossy sweetbriar, rather delicate plant.

R. eglanteria robusta: luxuriant, fragrant double sweetbriar, flowering abundantly from June until September.

R. eglanteria marmorea: marble-flowered sweetbriar.

R. eglanteria rubra: red-flowered sweetbriar. It resembles some of the smaller species of centifolia, not so fragrant in the foliage as other sweetbriars. It blooms from July until October.

. . . and found

Humphrey Brooke, owner of the most remarkable and extensive private collection of old roses in Britain at Claydon† in Suffolk, recently discovered a 'lost' hybrid perpetual that was growing on the church at Woolverstone, in Suffolk. The bush itself was over a hundred years old but still flowering. Brooke describes it as having the strongest scent of any rose he knows. A blind friend once 'put his nose in a bloom and said that if this scent was available in a bottle, it would put every tart in Europe out of business'.

The Woolverstone Church Rose is now back in limited commercial circulation under the name Surpassing Beauty of Woolverstone.

†Lime Kiln at Claydon – described by a French journalist as 'n'est pas une roseraie. C'est un jungle de roses' – is open to the public during the summer months.

Old Roses: a family tree

The development of the vividly coloured, large-bloomed, repeat-flowering 'hybrid teas' that now dominate the commercial rose market began about twenty years after Dean Hole's celebrated book first appeared. Before then, what are now known as shrub or old-fashioned roses had a fascinating history in which wild species and serendipitous crosses played important roles. The best-known were:

Gallicas – the first cultivated roses. Originated in W. Asia, but brought to Europe almost certainly before the tenth century BC. *R. gallica* '*officinalis*' is the famous Red Rose of Lancaster, otherwise known as the Apothecaries' Rose.

Other historic varieties include: Rosa Mundi, with red and white striped petals; Cardinal de Richelieu, deep violet; Belle Isis, flesh pink.

A single flowering season, as in the next four groups.

Damasks – very fragrant group. First came from naturally occurring crosses between *R. gallica* and *R. phoenicia* (a very floriferous wild rambler from the Middle East). In England by 1520.

Famous old varieties, all soft pink: Marie Louise, Kazanlik (source of Attar of Roses), Celsiana, Omar Khayyam (found growing on the tomb of this Persian poet in 1890, taken to Kew for propagation, and later planted out on the Suffolk tomb of his translator Edward Fitzgerald).

Albas – *R. alba*, the White Rose of York, probably came here with the Romans and may be a cross between the damask and the wild dog-rose, *R. canina*.

Maiden's Blush (pre-fifteenth century), Félicité Parmentier (1836).

Centifolias – the very double 'cabbage' roses often seen in Dutch paintings. Probably a complex cross between damask, dog and musk (*R. moschata*) hybrids.

Fantin Latour, blush-pink, quartered blooms; Tour de Malakoff, dark mauve-pink.

Moss roses – sports of the Centifolias, in which sepals and flower stalks are covered in hair-like mossy growth. Originated in mid seventeenth century.

White Moss (1735), Willy Lobb, lilac.

Bourbons – repeat flowering roses appear at last because of continuous flowering China roses (*R. chinensis*) being brought into the breeding line. First recorded early nineteenth century on the Ile de Bourbon near Madagascar, as a result of chance crosses between the damasks and Chinas the French settlers used to make hedges from. Can flower up to Christmas, with globular, rich, fruit-scented blooms.

La Reine Victoria, pink; Boule de Neige, pure white, Variegata de Bologna, white with purple striping.

Hybrid perpetuals – the link between old and modern roses. A very disparate group largely resulting from seedlings produced by chance insect crosses between all the above groups. More than 4000 named varieties between 1837 and 1900, including:

General Jacqueminot, rich rosy-scarlet, exceptionally fragrant;

Old garden furniture

Vanished along with many of the old roses are many of the artefacts they used to climb around: gazebos, pergolas, cupolas – and for that matter all manner of traditional garden furniture. Not many gardens nowadays will have scope for a grand mound or artificial mount, surmounted by a banqueting house, or a dovecote in the old style, housing upwards of 500 pairs of pigeons and bigger than the average country cottage of the present day. However, even in a moderately small space you can take traditional ideas of garden-making and modify them to your own needs. If you can't cope with a large mound, with alleys and fruit trees, why not a small rise with one or two decorative small trees, or even a bank covered with herbs and flowers to please the eye, with maybe a bench set into it. Dovecotes today are purely for the pleasure of seeing and hearing these attractive birds, so you need to think in terms of several pairs of dainty white fantails or perhaps one of the more unusual breeds, such as the archangel or jacobin, and a correspondingly smaller dovecote. Sundials were in use long before the division of the day into twenty four hours was adopted in the fifteenth century. Clearly, they are nowadays decorative rather than functional but a properly constructed sundial may be expected to give the time accurately to the nearest minute. The most common kind is set horizontally with its calibration dependent on the direction of the sun, but there are also cylindrical dials (which are easier to construct) and altitude dials which work on the variation of the sun's changing height and direction of the sun (these may require adjustment to the time of year). Andrew Marvell's sundial consisted of a round bed of herbs, each segment representing an hour:

How well the skilful gardener drew
Of flowers and herbs this deal new,
Where from above the milder sun
Does through a fragrant zodiac run;
And, as it works, the industrious bee
Computes its time as well as we.
How could such sweet and wholesome
    hours
Be reckoned but with herbs and
    flowers!

From 'The Garden'

Common moss rose

folk, who has a list of more than 700, including some exceptionally rare Victorian tea roses and Boursault roses (hybrids based on the beautiful European Alpine rose, *R. penduli-na*). Peter Beales also follows the time-honoured tradition of following up the chance seedlings that occur in

---

For an exhaustive account of the history of roses, see Gerd Krüssman's epic Roses,* *which includes a detailed dictionary of over 1300 varieties and comprehensible accounts of do-it-yourself hybridization.*

Emperor du Maroc, dark, almost black blossoms; Souvenir du Docteur Jamain, exquisitely formed flowers, wine-red.

An increasing number of old-fashioned roses are coming on to the market, and most dealers stock a few varieties. Far and away the largest collection is at **Peter Beales*** in Nor-

his beds. The most remarkable (now on the market) is Anna Pavlova, dark-leaved, and with thickly scrolled pink flowers whose astonishing scent suggests a strong Bourbon influence. One writer was quite overcome: 'It is quite haunting; the nearest I can get to describing it would be to imagine a picnic of fresh fruit salad, topped with Turkish Delight, and served under a flowering May tree!' – and he was not exaggerating.

Directory

Books

Genders, Roy, *Collecting Antique Plants* (Pelham Books, 1971).

Gibson, Michael, *Shrub Roses, Climbers and Ramblers* (Collins, 1981).

Jekyll, Gertrude (many of her enormous output of books are now being republished by the Antique Collectors Book Club).

Krüssmann, Gerd, *Roses* (Batsford, 1981).

Perring, F. H. & Farrell, L. (ed.) *The British Red Data Book: 1 Vascular Plants* (Society for the Promotion of Nature Conservation, 1977).

Robinson, William, *The English Flower Garden* (1883).

Robinson, William, *The Wild Garden* (1870).

Scott-James, Anne, *The Cottage Garden* (Allen Lane, 1981).

Wells, Terry *et al*, *Creating Attractive Grasslands Using Native Plant Species* (Nature Conservancy Council, 1981), obtainable from NCC, Attingham Park, Shrewsbury, Salop.

Suppliers

David, Austin, Bowling Green Lane, Albrighton, Wolverhampton (old roses).

Avon Bulbs, Bathford, Bath (rare bulbs).

Peter Beales, Intwood Nurseries, Swardeston, Norwich (old roses).

Bressingham Gardens, Diss, Norfolk (cottage and herbaceous plants).

Beth Chatto, 'Unusual Plants', White Barn House, Elmstead Market, Nr Colchester, Essex (rare and unusual flowers).

Richard Cawthorne, 28 Elm Road, Sidcup, Kent (violas).

John Chambers, 15 Westleigh Road, Barton Seagrave, Kettering, Northamptonshire (wild flower seeds).

Emorsgate Seeds, Emorsgate, Terrington St Clement, King's Lynn, Norfolk (wild flower seeds).

Jackson, J. A., Post Office Nurseries, Kettlehulme, Whaley Bridge, Stockport, Lancashire (violas).

Margery Fish Nurseries, East Lambrook Manor, East Lambrook, South Petherton, Somerset (cottage flowers).

John Mattock, Nuneham
Courtenay, Oxford (old roses).

McMurtie, Mrs, The Rock Garden
Nursery, Balbithar House,
Kintore, Inverurie,
Aberdeenshire (old cottage
flowers).

Mary Mottram, Yardwell Cross,
North Molton, Devon (cottage
flowers, old and new).

Naturescape, Little Orchard,
Whatton-in-the-Vale,
Nottingham (wild flower seeds).

Oak Cottage Herb Farm, Nesscliffe,
Shrewsbury, Shropshire (old
cottage plants).

Suffolk Herbs (see *Herbs*).

Paradise Centre, Twinstead Road,
Lamarsh, Bures, Suffolk (bulbs
and tubers).

Ramparts Nurseries, Bakers Lane,
Colchester, Essex (pinks).

Societies

The Alpine Garden Society,
Secretary Mr E. M. Upward, Lye
End Link, St John's, Woking,
Surrey.

British Association of Rose
Breeders, 1 Bank Alley,
Southwold, Suffolk.

National Council for the
Conservation of Plants and
Gardens, c/o The Royal
Horticultural Society Garden,
Wisley, Woking, Surrey.

National Viola & Pansy Society, 16
George Street, Handsworth,
Birmingham 21.

North of England Pansy & Viola
Society, 27 Firavenue,
Ravensthorpe, Dewsbury,
Yorkshire.

Royal National Rose Society,
Chiswell Green, St Albans,
Hertfordshire.

VEGETABLES

The conservation of vegetable varieties is a matter of taste in a more literal sense than usual. But it's arguably the area where the needs are most urgent. We could get by, at a pinch, without pansies and parsley, but not without plant food crops. And with vegetables (on anyone's prediction) likely to be playing an increasingly important part in Western diet, we are going to need all the variety we can get: winter salads, spring fruit, vegetables rich in protein and fibre, roots big and starchy enough to carve like a joint of meat, vegetables for climbing on trellises and growing in window boxes, vegetables that will survive droughts and thrive on spoil tips. And that, of course, is to say nothing about flavours . . .

Vegetable sanctuaries

Because of their overall policy of standardization the EEC has prohibited the marketing of any variety of vegetable that isn't properly registered. Since this is a long and expensive process involving field trials as well as the complex process of registration itself, it is only economically viable with varieties that are likely to have a wide public appeal – i.e. those that are already known and popular (and usually rather bland). Vegetables whose appeal is more limited (often simply because they are unfamiliar) are apt to go to the wall, along with their suppliers in many cases. But the EEC hasn't yet made it illegal to grow or give away unregistered vegetable varieties, and over the last few years a number of 'vegetable sanctuaries' have sprung up to save threatened old types from extinction.

They include:
- *Dean's Court* at Wimborne in Dorset. Specialities include the Stoke lettuce, a direct descendant of the cos lettuce brought back by the Crusaders from the Greek island of Kos and for the last 150 years grown on by just one family.
- *Styal Country Park*, near Manchester
- *Bishop's Palace*, Wells, Somerset
- *The National Vegetable Research Station* at Wellesbourne in Warwickshire, which with a grant from Oxfam is building up a seed bank that will eventually house some 15,000 varieties. The bulk of the seeds are kept in a sophisticated cold store at −20°C. and near zero humidity. Batches are grown on from time to time to

Lost

Remember when radishes were big, spicy *and* crisp?

Wood's Early Frame Radish . . . The roots, which are of a very elongated-ovoid shape, are usually from 2, 2/5 to 2, 4/5 inches long, and about 4/5 inch broad in the thickest part, which is not far below the base of the leaf-stalks. The skin is of a very lively carmine red, which becomes gradually paler towards the lower end of the root. The flesh is very white, firm, juicy, very crisp, fresh and pleasant to the taste, with a slightly pungent flavour . . .

Not a blurb from a seed packet but a quote from the seminal *The Vegetable Garden*, Vilmorin-Andrieux, 1885.

Nettle-leaved Canterbury kidney bean, from The Vegetable Garden, *by Vilmorin-Andrieux, 2nd ed, 1905.*

Some of the old varieties of vegetable that are now unobtainable commercially:

Ragged Jack kale – dark, purplish foliage which looks as if it has been eaten by caterpillars. Prolific, even during the hardest winters.

Black Canterbury kidney bean – a pod bean, listed by William Robinson early this century. The pods are an intense dark green and very long. The black seeds aren't used, but are removed before cooking the tender and very flavourful pods.

Soldier bean – famous for a blotch whose silhouette resembles a palace guard. One of the original American baking beans.

English wonder pea – raised by a Mr Tipping in Kenilworth around 1880. Very dwarf (about 14 inches max) and with a prolonged cropping period.

Up-to-date onion – large and fiery, specifically bred to go with bread, cheese and beer. Highly resistant to downy mildew.

The Altrincham carrot – very old, very long (often 20 inches) and very tender. It is also almost without the woody core which mars many modern carrots (but which unfortunately makes it liable to break under mechanised harvesting).

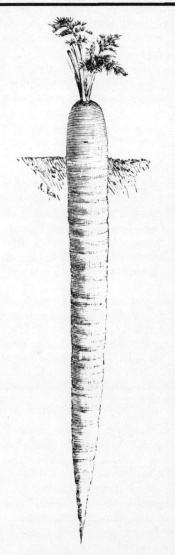

The Altrincham carrot, from The Vegetable Garden, *by Vilmorin-Andrieux, 2nd ed, 1905.*

check their viability and to in-
crease the stock of seeds, and
cross and back-breeding experiments carried out.

Although seed storage is no
substitute for conservation of liv-
ing plants, growing and evolving
in a real and changing environ-
ment, it does guard against the
possibility of complete extinction
of a variety because of, say, freak
climatic conditions or disease.
The director of the seed bank is
enthusiastic about the practical
contribution some obsolete varieties might make; for example,
the local Vale of Evesham Brus-
sels sprouts, which flourished for
centuries free of disease to a de-
gree that seems to have been lost
in modern varieties (which are
bred largely for size and early harvesting).

The inspiration (and most of
the initial seed material), for the

vegetable sanctuaries came from
Lawrence Hills' **Henry Doubleday Research Association***
(founded in 1954 and now the
largest body of organic gardeners
in Britain). Its members are able
to join what amounts to a vegetable 'seed library' scheme. They
are 'lent' seeds by the Association, grow them on, save the seed,
and then at the end of the season
return some of this to the library
together with a report on how well
the variety has done.

On the expanding catalogue of
vegetables on loan are La Lollo
lettuce and Pen-y-byd marrow,
both of which the EEC has made
it illegal to sell:

- La Lollo: a bizarrely beautiful
Italian 'flower lettuce', with
crinkled, purple-tinged leaves
stacked like a pagoda, that can be
repeatedly snipped off ('cut and
come again'). It's a marvellous
multiple purpose plant that could
theoretically be sold as a flower –
but not as a vegetable.

- Pen-y-byd (Top o' the world)
Marrow: the true Welsh marrow,
of very ancient pedigree, with
round pale fruits. Has the genetic
ability to grow in colder and wet-
ter climates than many marrow
varieties – in fact in the kind of
summers we look likely to have
more of in the future.

Piss-a-bed

*It's worth remembering that the
Victorian gentry's belief in dandelion's
efficacy at 'flushing out the kidneys'
was not entirely wishful thinking. The
plant has proven powers as a mild
diuretic and laxative, as testified by
many of its local names. (Though these
aren't as great as was believed by a
family we knew in Suffolk, whose
twin daughters were made to wash
their hands after picking dandelion
leaves for their tortoises.)*

The HDRA is eager for new members to join the seed library scheme –
particularly gardeners who are pre-

pared to take on single varieties ('seed guardians') – and so avoid the possibility of cross-breeding.

It is also always on the look out for scarce and obsolete seed varieties to add to its stock, and would be glad to hear from any reader who has, for example, old packets of seed of varieties no longer on general sale; or who is growing unusual varieties and is prepared to donate seed.

Vegetable seed

Good husewifes in Sommer will save
  their owne seedes,
Against the next yere, so occasion nedes
One sede for another, to make exchange
With fellowlie neighbourhood, seemeth
  not strange.

> Thomas Tusser, *Five Hundred Points
> of Good Husbandry*, 1573

A fact little advertised by seed merchants is that many kinds of seed will keep over until the next year or beyond. Lawrence Hills, taking the mantle of Thomas Tusser four centuries before, wrote a thrifty poem on the subject.

You have in your drawer since
  Candlemas Day,
All the seed packets you daren't throw
  away,
Seed Catalogue cometh as year it doth
  end,
But look in ye drawer before money you
  spend.

Throw out ye Parsnip, 'tis no good next
  year,
And Scorzonera if there's any there,
For these have a life that is gone with ye
  wynde
Unlike all ye seeds of ye cabbagy kinde.

Broccoli, Cauliflower, Sprouts, Cabbage
  and Kale,
Live long like a farmer who knoweth
  good ale:
Three years for certain, maybe five or
  four,
To sow in their seasons they stay in ye
  drawer.

Kohl-Rabi lasts with them and so does
  Pei-Tsai,
The winter 'cos-lettuce' to sow in July,
But short is the life of ye Turneps and
  Swedes
Sow next year only, enough for your
  needs.

Mustard and Cress for when salads come
  round,
Sows for three seasons so buy half a
  pound,
Radish lasts four years, both round ones
  and long,
Sown thinly and often they're never too
  strong.

Last year's left Lettuce sows three
  summers more,
And Beetroot and Spinach-beet easily
  four,
But ordinary Spinach, both prickly and
  round,
Hath one summer left before gaps waste
  ye ground.

Leeks sow three Aprils and one hath
  gone past,
And this is as long as ye Carrot will last,
Onion seed keeps till four years have
  flown by,
But sets are so easy and dodge onion-fly.

Store Marrows and Cucumbers, best
  when they're old,
Full seven summers' sowings a packet
  can hold.
Six hath ye Celery that needs a frost to
  taste,
So hath Celeriac before it goes to
  waste.

Broad Beans, French ones, Runners,
  sown in May,
Each hath a sowing left before you throw
  away,
And short Peas, tall Peas, fast ones and
  slow,
Parsley and Salsify have one more spring
  to sow.

Then fillen ye form that your seedsmen
  doth send,
For novelties plentie, there's money to
  spend,
Good seed and good horses are worth the
  expense,
So pay them your poundies as I paid my
  pence.

From *Grow Your Own Fruit and
Vegetables*,* Lawrence D. Hills
With grateful acknowledgement to
the author.

Preserving your own

To save seed from your own vegetables, allow a few specimens to
flower and on a dry day place cel-
lophane bags over the unripe seed-
heads. Tie securely, but not too
tightly round the stalk. When the
head appears to be fully dry, bend

Amateur Veg

Despite their own vast facilities for
breeding, nurseries and seedsmen
do occasionally take on varieties
raised or discovered by amateurs.
Hammonds Dwarf Scarlet, the
first true dwarf form of the runner
bean, was a natural mutation of the
variety Prizewinner discovered by
an amateur gardener, William
Hammond of Hounslow in 1954.
He sent it to the seed merchants,
Unwins, who developed it to
commercial quality and introduced
it as 'the most outstanding
vegetable novelty for half a
century'. Unfortunately,
unexpected deterioration in stock
has kept this variety off the market
for 1983, but this is only one of
many new varieties submitted by
private gardeners which this seed
company has marketed. One of
their best broad beans, Red
Epicure, was also raised by an
amateur (as, incidentally, are most
of their sweet peas). If you think
you have a likely candidate, grow
it on for two or three years to make
sure that it grows true to form and
then send it to one of the seed firms.

---

the stalk over, cut the seed head off,
and shake the seed free into the bag.
If you wish to avoid cross-breeding
(on self-fertile flowers) place the bags
over the flower-heads *before* the buds
have opened.

Clean the seed by any combination

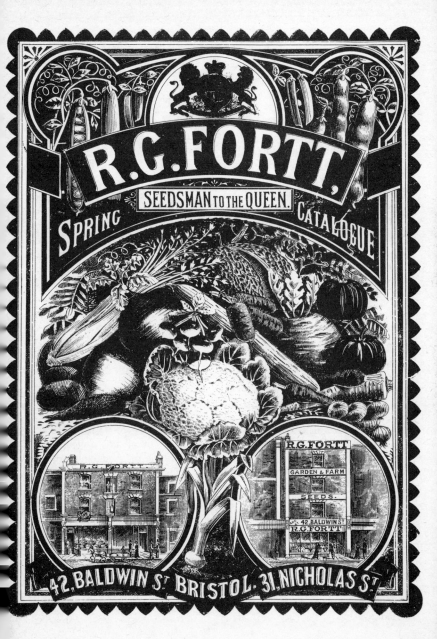

of sieving, winnowing and blowing you fancy, but don't wash them. Transfer them to envelopes, seal and label well, not forgetting to add the date of harvesting and the origins of the seed from which you grew them. (You can also use self-sealing plastic bags or old coin bags. Seal the latter with 3M tape and write name, etc, on this with a ball-point pen.) Then store the envelopes in a cool, but above all, *dry* place. Don't put them in a fridge or freezer, both of which have highly humid atmospheres.

Less usual vegetables

Dandelion, *Taraxacum officinale*. Jack Boyce, a Cambridgeshire nurseryman, has told us the story of the dandelion's first time round as a salad herb:

When times were very bad in this district it was quite usual for families to go out and dig dandelion roots up in the fields, the wild ones, and sell them to the chemist to get money to buy bread.

But also, particularly in the 1880s, it was customary for the gentry to grow dandelions in their unheated greenhouses for winter salads. As you know they are very beneficial for flushing out the kidneys, and helped the rich port drinking inhabitants from getting gout. Dandelion salads were very popular in those days . . . also sandwiches of thin brown bread and butter filled with dandelion leaves were served by the ladies for afternoon tea.

My father was very friendly with the well-known Snell family who ran the famous Royal Nurseries in Broad Street,

Ely, and they used to supply dandelion seed and plants to the local gentry. . . . The demand has grown to require more seed than we could produce, so now the seed is grown on contract in France and imported. Over the years a great deal of work has gone into producing a cultivated form of dandelion so that the leaves are larger and more pleasant to eat than the wild form.

(Large-leaved form seeds available from **J. W. Boyce**,★ **Thompson and Morgan**.★)

There are all manner of ways of making the wild form itself more acceptable (though you may find its astringent bitterness its most attractive feature).

Pick young leaves, for a start, before May. Pick them regularly, to ensure a continual flush of new greenery. Try blanching the leaves by growing them up through the inside of a toilet roll. And bring roots indoors in the winter, for forcing out-of-season salads, just as the Victorians did. (There is a good account of how to do this in Euell Gibbons' excellent *Stalking the Healthful Herbs*.★ And don't forget to add a few dandelion flowers to your green salad, for colour, and for an intriguing, sweet and sour contrast in flavours.

Purslane, *Portulaca oleracea*, annual. Introduced into Britain in the Middle Ages, popular as a pickle and salad vegetable but can also be eaten lightly steamed or boiled with butter. Fleshy leaves on red stems.

Fat Hen, *Chenopodium album,* annual. A Neolithic vegetable. A fidget to gather the stem tops and leaves but delicious lightly steamed and served with butter. Field edges and overgrown gardens are good sources.

Burnet, *Poterium, species,* perennial. Used to be a common salad herb. The variety usual in cultivation, *P. officinalis,* has larger leaves than the native *P. sanguisorba.* The leaves of both species are cucumber-scented.

Burnet, from The Vegetable Garden.

Skirrit, *Sium sisarum*, perennial. A plant of Chinese origin, long cultivated in Europe – a sweet, aromatic root vegetable; according to Worlidge 'the sweetest, whitest and most pleasant of roots'. Eat boiled or steamed and served with butter. Available from enterprising seedsmen.

Rampion, *Campanula rapunculus*, perennial. Related to the harebell. White sweetish roots which were popular both raw and cooked, up until the early nineteenth century. Went out of favour, as did so many roots, as the potato became widely available.

Rocket, *Eruca sativa*, annual. A member of the cabbage family, with the above-ground growth of a radish. Much spicier than most salad herbs, and very popular up to the late eighteenth century.

Seeds of all the above available from **John Chambers,*** and **Suffolk Herbs.***

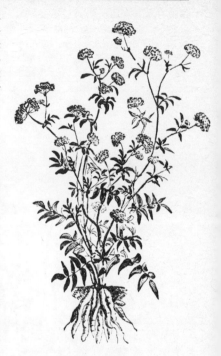

Skirret, from The Vegetable Garden.

Wanted – a perennial parsley

Parsley seeds are maddeningly difficult to germinate and the plants irresistibly attractive to slugs in their youth. It's normally a biennial, but some of the wild or naturalized colonies in Britain by the sea are very well established and there may be perennial clones amongst them. Keep looking!

Winter Salads

The red Italian chicories, such as Red Verona, add wonderful colour to a winter salad, their own colours changing from greeny brown to deeper and deeper red as winter progresses. Some varieties form beautiful nugget heads like miniature red cabbages. If these are cut, leaving the roots in the ground, further leaves will shoot up for many months. . . . To me the delight of winter salads lies in blending a range of plants, and savouring a variety of flavours, colours and textures, using just a simple French dressing of oil and vinegar: many other plants can be added to those described above: rocket, Japanese greens Mizuna (both of which stand several degrees of frost), shredded red and green cabbage, the whole range of seeds which can be sprouted indoors (such as mung and adzuki beans and lentils), mustard and cress, the young shoots of salsify, dandelion and so on . . .

Joy Larkcom (author of *Salads the Year Round*), *The Countryman*, Autumn 1979

Like London buses, lettuces seem always to come at once however hard you try to stagger their growth periods. Salad Bowl is a delicious lettuce in itself and has the advantage of not hearting up. You pick leaves from the outside of the plant all through the season – even through the winter from some hardy specimens.

The sloth's vegetable garden

Many of the older vegetable varieties, especially those that aren't too distant from their wild ancestors, are perennial – which raises the seductive possibility of an entirely perennial vegetable garden, which will need no more hard digging and

Future Veg

Most enterprising of the established seed merchants are **Thompson and Morgan**★ of Ipswich, who in a splendid and discursive annual catalogue regularly announce unusual new vegetables for amateur growers. In recent years they have introduced Desiree stringless runner beans, Pacemaker beetroots (a hybrid with sweet sugarbeet parentage), Shamrock Big Apple cabbage, miniature cauliflowers, Fembaby windowsill cucumber, Monoppa spinach (with a low oxalic acid content), Pixie tomatoes (frost resistant) and vegetable spaghetti.

Deleted (temporarily, we hope)

Thompson and Morgan frequently run up against the restrictions imposed by the EEC against free marketing of seed varieties. In 1980, for instance, more than twenty new vegetables in their catalogue were not permitted to be sold, including:

Bina – a dwarf runner bean that needs no climbing support.

Self-wrap cauliflower – leaves curl over the head and help prevent yellowing in the sun.

Alma celery – self blanching.

Hemed-Ogen melon – resistant to mildew and wilt.

Spartan sleeper onion – can be stored for at least sixteen months after lifting.

finnicky attention than a hardy flower border. Just pick sparingly from each plant when you fancy, heap plenty of manure or compost on the bed each winter, and you should be able to go on harvesting without replanting for several years.

The scenario

Plant sea-kale (available from **Thompson and Morgan**) in the centre, and use surrounding vegetables to help blanch the young stems in the way that shingle and sand were once used on wild stock.

Close to it, use two or three plants of a perpetual spinach-beet, or best of all sea-spinach, *Beta maritima* (often sea-kale's companion on beaches), grown from wild seed.

On not being a vegetable
In the village of Milden in Suffolk, they have put up a huge metal statue of Fat Hen (see page 77) whose Anglo-Saxon name melde *gave the village its name.*

Vegetables rarely get that kind of respect, or have their good looks shown off in potagers. Remember your vegetables have been occupying your garden for months before you use them (and other people's gardens for centuries) and spare a thought for their non-utilitarian qualities.

NB: Parkinson mentions that gentlewomen gathered carrot leaves for their beauty and stuck them into their hats or pinned them to the arms of their dresses instead of feathers.

Around them place smaller green veg – sorrel (use the wild English variety, not the more insipid French or buckler-leaved varieties) and the kale-flavoured Good King Henry. And so that the garden isn't dominated by greens, scatter amongst these a few globe artichokes, some tree onions (*Allium cepa*) from the tops of whose stalks bunches of sharp, shallot-sized onions can be picked in mid-summer, and some Bath asparagus (*Ornithogalum pyrenaicum*), available from specialist bulb merchants. This is a native woodland plant in parts of England, a lily like the true asparagus, but less fussy in its requirements. The flowering shoots are cut and treated exactly as true asparagus and used to be gathered for sale from the limestone countryside around Bath before the Theft Act of 1968 (see page 103).

Potagers

Alternatively, whether planning a new garden or recreating an old, why not adapt from our French friends and create a *potager*? They have a genius for making the useful decorative, and the *potager*, though providing food for the pot, is no mere vegetable patch. In essence, it is a concentration of vegetables, fruit and flowers in a pleasing symmetrical pattern. . . .

The all-important outline of the pattern should be of one material only, for unity and permanence. Box, 9 in. to 1 ft high, is still best. It also stops ground draughts so crops inside grow better. Lemon thyme, hyssop, dwarf lavender and santolina are also good.

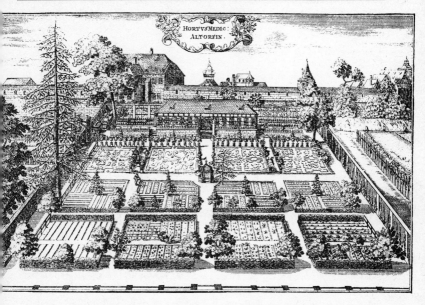

The seventeenth-century Altdorf University herb and vegetable garden.

Within these 'frames' a great variety of crops could be grown according to the owner's fancy. One could simply fill them with strawberries – a sixteenth century idea; or potatoes in two diagonally opposed beds and French beans in the others, to start with at least . . . Our modest *potager*'s four quarters could perhaps be made up from: Bluey cabbages and 'Solaise' leeks and silvery broad beans; green parsley, sorrel, saladings, chives, seakale beet, peas, carrots; yellow spinach beet, Butterhead lettuces, Poitou leeks, golden self-blanching celery; red chard, beetroot and cabbages, pinky ornamental cabbages and ruddy-leaved lettuces.

Shirley Martell, *The Countryman*,
Summer 1977

Try vertical ornamentation, too, with standard gooseberry bushes, beans and courgettes trained up trellis work – or up espalier fruit trees.

Directory

Books

Furner, Brian, *The Kitchen Garden* (Pan, 1966).

Gibbons, Euell, *Stalking the Healthful Herbs* (New York, 1966).

Gibbons, Euell, *Stalking the Wild Asparagus* (New York, 1962).

Grigson, Jane, *Jane Grigson's Vegetable Book* (Michael Joseph, 1978).

Harrison, S. G. *et al*, *The Oxford Book of Food Plants* (OUP, 1969).

Hartley, Dorothy, *Food in England* (Macdonald, 1954).

Hills, Lawrence, *Grow your own Fruit and Vegetables* (Faber, 1979).

Larkcom, Joy, *Salads the Year Round* (Hamlyn, 1982).

Lovelock, Yann, *The Vegetable Book* (Allen & Unwin, 1972).

Mabey, Richard, *Food for Free* (Fontana, 1975).

Suppliers

Boyce, J. W., 67 Station Road, Soham, Ely, Cambridgeshire.

Chambers, John (see *Flowers*).

Chiltern Seeds, Sunnymede Avenue, Chesham, Buckinghamshire.

Suffolk Herbs (see *Herbs*).

Suttons Seeds, Hele Road, Torquay, Devon.

Thompson and Morgan, London Road, Ipswich, Suffolk.

I. & S. Unwin Ltd, Oldfield Lane, Wisbech, Cambridgeshire.

Societies

The Henry Doubleday Research Association, Convent Lane, Bocking, Braintree, Essex.

FRUIT

People have been actively occupied with raising fruit for many centuries and good new varieties have come alike from great and modest gardens: Ribston Pippin originated in the great grounds at Ribston Hall; a small garden in Nottinghamshire grew Bramley and another near Slough in Buckinghamshire owned by a retired brewer called Richard Cox gave us today's best-loved eating apple.

Now, perhaps more than at any other period, amateur gardeners have a great part to play in ensuring the continuation of old varieties of fruit (and the discovery of new types bred from them) as increasing pressures are placed upon commercial nurseries to look to market standardization and immediate profit.

For the gardener, there is still a good range of traditional varieties for sale from specialist nurseries of the four most popular tree fruits: apple, pear, plum and cherry. But soft fruits fare less well. Even the fifty or so varieties of gooseberry still available from specialist nurseries are only a pale reflection of past riches. For many reasons (of which virus infection is an important one) it is almost impossible to find old kinds of strawberry apart from the renowned

Royal Sovereign and the Alpines. Of the raspberry only Lloyd George and Golden Everest survive, but in the currants, red, white and black, there are quite a few old varieties.

First fruit

The chief ancestor of all cultivated apples is the European wild crab *Malus sylvestris*. This occurs in at least two forms; the north European 'crab', with sour, shiny, green fruit and smooth leaves; and a sub-species from S. Europe, which has sweeter, yellow or pink-tinged fruit and downy leaves. As well as being highly variable in themselves, these two forms hybridize, and it was from their better fruited seedlings that the first apples were selected for cultivation. (Later, as many as ten Asian

---

For historical background and descriptions (and availability) of tree fruit and soft fruit see F. Greenoak, Forgotten Fruits.★

All important details of pollination partners and incompatibilities are to be found in good catalogues and in Harry Baker's two excellent RHS books on fruits.★

species were brought into the breeding line.)

Because they cross-breed so readily, apples must be propagated by grafting (page 96) if they are to stay true. Most wilding apples (chance seedlings with at least one cultivated parent – most 'wild' apples are these, not true crabs) have small and rather sour fruit. But every so often there is a beneficial cross or throwback and an exciting new apple appears. These can crop up anywhere. Lane's Prince Albert originated in Berkhamsted, Hertfordshire. Henry Lane named it so as he planted out the seedling after cheering the Queen and Prince Albert through the town in 1841. Granny Smith reputedly grew from an Australian woman's compost heap; the Keswick Codlin from rubbish at Ulverston Castle; Shaw's Pippin from a seedling on Wheathampstead tip in Hertfordshire. So it's worth giving a chance to any seedlings that spring up in your garden, provided you have the space.

Voyage of Discovery

One of the best, if not the best early apple, has appeared only recently on the market. Like many of the old favourites, Discovery, as its name suggests, was the result of chance rather than scientific breeding.

It was a seedling from a Worcester Pearmain apple whose pips were sown by Mr Dummer of Langham, Essex in 1949 at the bottom of his garden. It grew into a likely tree and he decided to transplant it to a good position in his lawn. But as he was one-armed he needed help to replant it. Unfortunately, Mrs Dummer broke her ankle just at the point of planting, and during the weeks in which she recovered from this accident, Discovery lay on the lawn covered only with sacking to protect it from the frost. More in hope than any real expectation, the Dummers planted it. Not only did the tree survive, but it began to produce some fine fruit, news of which reached Mr Jack Matthews of the famous wholesale fruit-growing firm of Matthews. He first saw the tree on 13th September 1961, and though it was in a rather neglected condition as Mr Dummer had died in the meantime, he was sufficiently impressed to take a few grafts. The next year, he went to see the tree at its peak on 24th July, ate some of the excellent fruit and took more grafting material.

From then on the story was one of increasing success. The apple was eventually named Discovery and Matthews made arrangements to propagate and promote it. Fruit-growers went to view the original tree and bought the new apple in commercial quantities. Matthews now sells Discovery in thousands and its fruit ranks fourth in popularity. It is a handsome apple, crisp and sweet, ripening in July and through August, a time when there are not many good quality apples about – which probably accounts for the speed of its rise to success. Its parentage is not definitely known, but from its appearance it seems likely that the pollinator was Beauty of Bath.

Old apples

Since cultivation began an enormous number of varieties of apple have been raised. Muriel Smith's epic work, *The National Apple Register* lists no less than 6000 variety names together with history and probable parentage. How many of these still exist it would be impossible to guess, but only a few dozen are cultivated commercially.

These are some of the choicer old varieties:

Margil Highly flavoured apple of superb quality, ready for eating from October to January. A small tree, ideal for smallish gardens. Apples are pale primrose with a ruddy flush and overlaid with russet. Known in England before 1750.

Orleans Reinette First described in 1776, a favourite of fruit connoisseur Edward Bunyard. Gold-yellow with a slight flush of red and russet patches. The tree grows strongly upwards and outwards. It tastes very crisp, sweet and juicy. Good eating up until February.

White Transparent A taste of champagne in late July. A sparkling apple with a welcome touch of sharpness. It came to England in the mid-1800s from the Balkans or Russia. Colour greenish, ripening to palest milky-yellow. A fertile, vigorous tree, and among the earliest to crop.

James Grieve A continuing favourite: the colour of Cornish cream, flushed and striped red, tasting juicy and tender, ready for eating during September and October. Introduced by James Grieve about 1890, the tree is upright and vigorous.

Irish Peach Irish, as its name suggests, this apple was introduced to England about 1820. A delicious early variety, ready in August, it is small and pale yellow in colour with milky red streaks.

Gravenstein The known history of this apple goes back to 1669 when it arrived in Denmark. There are three different versions of its actual origins, but all sources are agreed that it is a splendid dessert apple. Orange-gold with a red flush, aromatic, crisp and tender within. It was introduced to England about 1760.

Norfolk Biffins – lost?

A huge, hard, sweet variety with a firm, rose-flushed skin. Biffins were dried slowly in cooling bread ovens, and packed in layers with straw between. The result was a flat, muffin-shaped apple, dried – though it might be more accurate to say slow-cooked – with its skin intact. Origins obscure. Also known as Cat's Head, Bearfin, or Beefing.

Reinettes and (left) the Isle of Wight Pippin, and Ribston Pippin (right) from the Herefordshire Pomona.

Ribston Pippin Raised at Ribston Hall in Yorkshire at the beginning of the eighteenth century, this is one of the best flavoured and richest apples. It is yellow with a dull brown-red flush overlaid with russet. A late season apple, sweet and aromatic.

St Edmunds Pippin 'Quite the best early russet' according to Edward Bunyard, this apple was raised in Bury St Edmunds about 1870. A medium-sized tree of upright growth, it makes a good garden tree, producing its golden-russet apples in October and November.

Consult a good reference book or nursery about pollinators. Some apples require two.

Fruit tasting

Tastes differ and it is a long-term gamble to opt for a particular variety on the basis of what one writer or another has written in a catalogue or book. There is an opportunity to try for yourself at many orchards all over the country in early October when you can ring the **Apple and Pear Council*** and be given a list of orchards participating in the apple and pear tasting scheme.

If you have an old fruit tree and would like to know its name, the **Fruit Identification Department*** at Wisley are happy to attempt identification.

If you have a favourite fruit tree and would like more for yourself or to give away, certain nurseries will graft on to certified stock for you. (**New Tree Nurseries*** and **Scotts of Merriott***)

If you are keen to grow a variety not for sale but which is still grown at the National Fruit Trials, Scotts of Merriott 'can grow almost any kind in cultivation to order'.

Pears, plums and cherries

Although there is a wider choice of apples than any other fruit, there are specialist fruit nurseries which raise a good range of pear, cherry and plum varieties. It is arguable that a truly delicious pear needs to be home-grown; shop fruits suffer too much from bruising and early picking – and besides offer a very limited choice. Redoutable names and flavours from the past must include Beurre Hardy and Beurre Superfin, Winter Nelis and Josephine de Malines and Doyenne de Comice, raised in 1858 and still without peer.

Until a few years ago only those with very large gardens could hope to plant a cherry tree as it grows so large. Now the advent of 'Colt', a semi-dwarfing rootstock, has brought cherries within the scope of moderately sized gardens. They are choosy about their pollinators so if you plant only one tree, it has to be Morello or modern Stella – the only self-fertile sweet cherry – or if you are adventurous one of the old Amarelles. If you have room for more than one consider the hand-

Bees

The intensive farming practices which have brought about such drastic reductions in flower-rich pastures, hedgerow shrubs and flowering weeds look set to be self-defeating in at least one way. Because wild flowers have always been the principle source of food for bees, these important insects are having an increasingly thin time. Beekeepers report that nectar yields nationally have fallen by 50 per cent over the last ten years, and many have had to sell up. The bees themselves are undernourished, more prone to disease, and are declining in numbers.

The effect of this decline is already being felt by farmers and fruit growers. Orchard owners often have to import swarms from as much as a hundred miles away so that their flowers can be pollinated and the fruit set. The next crops to suffer will probably be legumes like broad beans and peas.

To help stop the decline, plant bee-plants in your garden. An excellent guide is *Garden Plants Valuable to Beekeepers*, published by the International Bee Research Association.

From 'The English Illustrated Magazine', c. 1890.

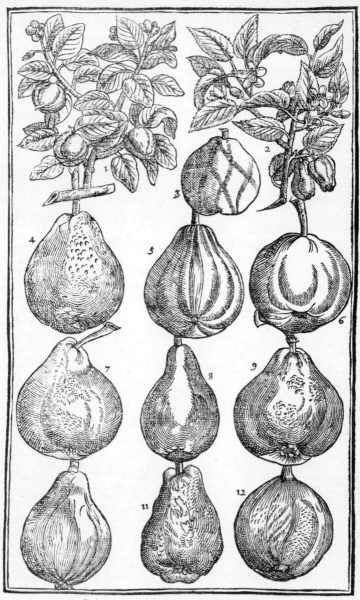

*Quince tree and fruit (1 and 3) and a pear tree,
and nine varieties popular in the early seventeenth century.*

some and sweet-tasting yellow Frogmore Early or the crimson Early Rivers or one of the Duke cherries halfway between sweet and tart, much loved by the gardeners of the past.

With plums there is an interesting choice of old varieties but once again care needs to be taken with pollinators. The gage group, unrivalled for flavour, is very particular, but a good Early Transparent Gage or Ouillins Golden Gage is worth the trouble. Coe's Golden Drop is as delicious as it sounds but needs care and is a shy cropper. Kirkes Plum is a good old dark plum. A large proportion of plums (especially damsons) used to be planted in (and gathered from) hedgerows, and this would be a nice tradition for the private gardener to reinstate. Farleigh Damson is readily available, as is the Myrobalan Plum which makes a thick, bushy hedge.

Ancient and unusual tree fruits

Gardening books of the seventeenth and eighteenth centuries contain instructions for cultivating a number of exotic fruits such as apricots, nectarines, peaches and almonds, and a few fruits which are difficult to buy commercially but which may be grown for oneself quite easily, such as medlars and quinces. Many of the old varieties are still available. No date is known for the Nottingham medlar or the pear-shaped quince but Moor Park apricot, introduced by Admiral Anson in 1760, first fruited at Moor Park, Hertford. A frequent quartet in old gardens was quince, medlar, mulberry and walnut, planted up at the four corners of the garden.

Fruit tree forms
Espalier apple and pear trees

It is possible to buy pre-shaped espaliers from nurseries, but it is much more fun and not difficult to make them for yourself. Not only do you tailor-fit your tree to its surroundings but you learn gradually in the process not to be afraid of pruning and shaping.

It is worth taking a bit of care with the support system as it will be there for a long while. Espaliers may be grown up walls, in which case horizontal wires ought to be placed 15 to 18 inches apart, one to support each tier of the espalier. In the *open* erect good strong posts every 12 to 18 feet and run the wires across them, bracing the end posts stoutly.

In early autumn dig over the soil for about 3 feet square and 18 inches deep, replace good topsoil and fertilize.

Note: Most apples and pears may be espaliered but beware 'tip-bearers' which will not fruit on heavily pruned twigs and 'triploid' types which are too vigorous for the espalier form. A good catalogue or nursery will give you information about these. For espalier rootstocks, see page 96.

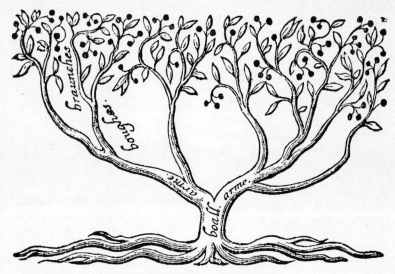

'The perfect form of a fruit tree', William Lawson,
A New Orchard and Garden, *1618.*

First year

- November to March: plant an un-feathered maiden tree (i.e. with buds not twigs) up to its soil mark, filling in with good soil and compost if you have it. Cut back the stem to within 15 inches from the ground (just above your first wire), noting three good buds, the lower two pointing in opposite directions.

- June to September: train the shoot from the uppermost bud vertically up a cane and the two others to the right and left, holding the canes initially at an angle of 45° to the main stem (tie canes to support wires to secure them).

- October to November: the first growing season ends. Take the two side branches down to the horizontal and secure them to the first tier wires. (Try Lawrence Hill's excellent tip of using old nylon stocking cut across into rings, as tree ties.) Cut back any other shoots of the main stem to three buds.

- Also cut back the central stem (leader) to just above your next wire (15 to 18 inches or so above the lower arms). Observe the two arms – you will probably need to prune them by about a third – taking them to a downward pointing bud, unless growth has been very thick and strong, in which case leave them unpruned.

Second and later years

- June to September: train the second tier of branches as you did the first. Also cut back the shoots from the main stem to three leaves and cut back the shoots from the horizontal arms in the same way to three leaves above the basal cluster of leaves.

- October to November: train and cut back the horizontal and vertical leaders as in the previous year.

  Continue this winter and summer pruning and training until the desired number of tiers has been achieved – usually three to five – but it can be more in very fertile soils with vigorous stocks.

- When your tree has reached its desired size and the trunk and tiered arms reach as far as you wish, simply prune the new terminal growth on the vertical and horizontal arms to origin each May. In summer (July) cut back the leaders again and cut back to three leaves the mature laterals growing away from the central stem, and cut back to basal leaves plus one leaf the laterals on the horizontal shoots.

Further tips

- Don't worry if one branch of your tiers is not doing as well as the other. If you raise the cane nearer to the vertical axis it should pick up.

- It is not a *disaster* if your toddler does a bit of pruning and rips off a branch or if you blunder into it one drunken evening with the same effect – trees are very obliging if you keep the soil good and give them a reasonable amount of care. If you lose a branch, simply select the nearest bud and train that one in its place. It may not be so perfectly symmetrical as your original but it will take an expert to see it, and it will fruit just as well.

- *Aftercare:* it is a good idea to mulch newly planted and young trees with rotted down manure, peat or compost. When the tree is established simply chew up the dead leaves with a Flymo. This provides worm-sized pieces which give the tree a good build-up of humus.

Other main forms

Such is the expertise that has been gathered over the centuries that a gardener nowadays can grow almost any kind of fruit tree in forms that will suit almost any garden. These are the main kinds:

Bush: stem of only 2 to 3 feet with branches rising to form a head; comes as dwarf bush (easily managed but aesthetically dull) and large bush giving good crops easily reached without ladders.

Standard and half-standard: main stem 6 or 4 feet in height before branching – suitable for larger gardens and orchards, good yield (and beautiful) if you have the room.

Half-standard

Full-standard

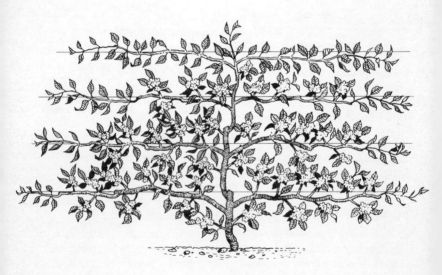

Four-tiered espalier

Spindlebush: (mostly apples) a cone-shaped tree with a single stem with branches off as near horizontal as possible to encourage heavy fruiting (about 7 to 8 feet). Good yield but awful shape.

Espalier: central stem with pairs of branches growing more or less opposite each other at right angles; very useful and decorative form; espaliers of three pairs of branches make useful garden dividers. Glorious archways of 12 or more pairs formed with multi-tiered espalies.

Cordons: single straight stem with restricted side growth, fruit spurs along the entire length, usually trained obliquely on support system. If you want lots of fruit in a small space you can plant these more closely than other forms but they are not handsome.

Pyramid and dwarf pyramid: Christmas tree shape, branches

Dwarf pyramid

radiating in diminishing length, may be closely grown for high cropping.

Single/double/triple cordons

A fan-trained fig.

Fan trained: branches trained to fan out from the base – especially popular for stone fruit (plums, peaches, cherries, apricots) up a high wall (or lower wall with trellis).

The Stock Market

The shape, size and time of first fruiting of your fruit trees depends very much upon which rootstock was used. Virtually no tree fruits are grown on their own roots: size, rate of growth and disease are much more controllable if a stock is used. Usually, you buy a tree ready grafted on to a selected stock and grown on for a couple of years. It is possible to buy rootstocks from some nurseries and

make your own graft, but remember that your own tree will take a bit longer to come to fruit.

Rootstocks and rough predictions of final size differ according to conditions:

Apples

M27: extremely dwarfing, good for pots and small gardens. Needs care with feeding and watering. Fairly new introduction, height 4 feet.

M9: very dwarfing. Requires good soil conditions and reasonable care. Bears fruit early (3 years) but root system brittle and the bush tree requires staking throughout its life;

6 to 10 feet in height and spread. (Also used for small espaliers, about 10 feet apart.)

M26: dwarf bush tree 8 to 12 feet in height and spread – needs staking for first 5 years. Suitable for small garden, tolerates average soil conditions. (Used for bush, dwarf pyramid, cordon, occasionally espalier or fan.)

MM106: semi-dwarfing, makes a bush tree 12 to 18 feet in height and spread, and has a wide soil tolerance. Trees usually produce fruit early – within 3 to 4 years. (Bush, spindlebush, cordon, espalier, fan.)

MM25: used by some nurseries to grow half-standards. Fairly vigorous, 16 to 18 feet height and spread.

MM111 and M2: vigorous medium to large trees depending on the soil conditions. (Bush, half-standard, standard, espaliers.) Slow to fruit compared with dwarfing stocks, 7 to 8 years.

Pears

Quince C: moderately vigorous – makes a bush pear tree 8 to 18 feet tall bearing fruit in 4 to 7 years. Not for poor soils (bush, cordon, dwarf pyramid and espalier). Best to make sure of virus free stock.

Quince A: slightly more vigorous than C – fruiting in 4 to 8 years.

Bush pears make trees between 10 and 20 feet in height and spread. Used for all forms except standards.

Pear stock: used for large standard trees. Very vigorous, making very large trees. Slow to bear fruit, but eventually giving heavy crops.

Plums

St Julien A: semi-dwarfing, 3 to 6 years for fruiting.

Pixy: more dwarfing but more difficult to obtain. Fruits in 3 to 6 years.

Brompton: large.

Myrobalan B: large and vigorous.

Cherries

Colt: usually extremely vigorous. Sweet cherries are often grown as a fan on a wall but even on semi-dwarfing stocks they grow moderately large. Most nurseries use Colt which may be grown as a fan or pyramid, bush or half-standard; height and spread 12 to 15 feet.

F12/1: grows vigorously to height of 18 to 24 feet, also used for large fans: for half-standards and standards allow 30 to 40 feet. Morellos and Amarelle type cherries are less vigorous and may reach about 12 to 15 feet on Colt and 15 to 18 feet on F12/1.

Family trees

A new name for an old practice. The Romans were skilled in grafting several varieties of fruit on to one stock and the practice is mentioned in some of the old English gardening books. It has come back into fashion with the realization that with a family apple, pear, plum or cherry you can get the luxury of several varieties in a small garden which would never be able to accommodate the same number of individual fruit trees. It is also extremely useful in the case of cherries and plums (which are choosy about their pollen partners and sometimes require two pollinators) if they are all growing together on one tree.

Many of the big seed merchants and nursery suppliers stock a couple of family trees, but there are places where much more exciting things are happening. A firm actually called **Family Trees*** does a tempting range of double and triple varieties as small trees on MM106 rootstock or as dual fans. The combinations are imaginative with many old varieties such as Gravenstein, Ashmead's Kernel and Bramley's seedling, Cornish Gillyflower, St Edmund's Pippin or the delectable Margil, Orleans Reinette and Irish Peach. There are also pear, plum, peach, nectarine and cherry 'dual fans'. **Deacons Nurseries*** situated on the Isle of Wight also has an excellent range of family trees.

Pruning family trees

The nurseryman Philip House of **Family Trees** has chosen his family tree duos and trios with an eye to growth, pruning and cross pollination, matching varieties of equal vigour. Despite this, one variety will sometimes make excessive growth during the early years. To correct this, remove complete shoots, keeping the centre fairly open. This is best done in winter or in July and will keep the tree balanced and free of any misplaced shoots.

Occasionally cropping happens eccentrically, with one variety setting an over-heavy crop, perhaps clusters of five or more fruits. These should be thinned down to one fruit per cluster or two where there are plenty of close leaves, and spaced about 4 to 6 inches apart for dessert apples, and 6 to 9 inches for cookers. Use sharp scissors or press off the fruitlet between thumb and finger, leaving the stalk behind.

Trees in tubs

If you lack space for a full-grown tree in your garden, or lack a garden, or perhaps simply want to experiment with some extra fruit trees – almost every kind of fruit can be grown in a container, a pot, tub, barrel, box or trough. So long as the container is well-drained and not too cumbersome to be moved when necessary, you may find yourself growing better fruit than if you had simply planted into the ground. You can make sure the tree has exactly the soil it prefers and similarly tailor watering and feeding to its needs. Feeding is necessary in the growing season since the roots can't wander off and find their own nutrients, and daily watering is needed in the summer. On the other hand, it is easier to protect a tub-growing tree from frost and predators and the extra care you give it will result in better fruit (though because of the limitation of size, not in such quantity as from a large open-grown tree).

For good advice on potting, repotting and culture consult Harry Baker on 'Fruit' in the *RHS Encyclopaedia of Gardens**. Some varieties he suggests as suitable for pot-growing are: Lord Derby with Lane's Prince Albert apples (cookers); Discovery with Sunset (dessert apples); Conference and Williams Bon Chretien pears. (Apples and pears need cross-pollination so you need two sorts.) Stella (the first self-compatible cherry – so it may be grown on its own); Brown Turkey fig; Peregrine peach; Pine Apple and Early Rivers nectarines. Victoria, Denniston's Superb and Ouillins Golden Gage plums are all self-fertile and may be pot-grown singly.

Fruit Follies 1

If you are growing small trees in tubs, try imitating the eighteenth-century conceit of serving your dessert fruit on the tree. It is easy enough to mount a small tub or pot on to a wheeled base and move the whole contraption to your guests' side for their inspection and selection.

Fruit Follies 2

We have one friend, a resourceful Gaul of the Asterix breed, who is always busy with some new project connected, ultimately, with the pleasures of the belly. . . . One day our daughter watched him tying wine bottles over several barely formed pears on the espalier pear tree. What was he doing? Well, the pears would grow and ripen in their individual greenhouses. Then he would break the stems and fill the bottles up with a mixture of syrup . . . and *marc*. At Christmas and New Year, his pear liqueur would cause a sensation – like a ship in a bottle, but much better, because the contents of these bottles would be drinkable.

Jane Grigson, *Good Things*,
Michael Joseph, 1971

Gooseberries

The story of the rise of the gooseberry from a humble, small and
rather sharp wild berry (native in
Britain, despite some gardeners' beliefs) to a sumptuous dessert fruit,
must be one of the great instances of
do-it-yourself plant breeding.

There is no record in Britain of the
introduction of any cultivated kinds,
nor of cultivation itself beginning before the sixteenth century. Yet by the
eighteenth century gooseberry grow-

*The variety Compton's Sheba's Queen, painted by Mrs A. I.
Witters in 1825.*

ing had become a cult amongst cottagers in the industrial north and Midlands, and by the beginning of the twentieth century as many as 2000 named varieties were in circulation. The garden historian Edward Hyams believed that 'English cottagers domesticated this plant by introducing it from the wild into their gardens'.

The great spur to continued improvement in size and variety were the gooseberry shows, in which individual berries were matched against one another weight for weight. (The gooseberry seems to have been an ideal subject for this improbable north country hobby, being unpretentious – some would say vulgar – hardy and capable of being grown in a very small space.)

Gooseberry shows are still held in August in a number of Cheshire villages (Lower Withington, Marton, Swettenham, Goostrey, Peover, Holme Chapel, and Park Gate). Although competition is fierce, the gooseberry-growing community is a cooperative one, and cuttings of best plants are freely exchanged. Some of the favourite show varieties – e.g. Firbob and Montrose – have been raised comparatively recently by a local grower, Frank Carter.

These old varieties are markedly different from most giant-sized fruit and vegetables in that they are exceptionally sweet, and edible as an uncooked dessert fruit. The fruit gourmet Edward Bunyard reckoned they were 'the fruit *par excellence* for ambulant consumption. The freedom of the bush [though they are called 'trees' by the Cheshire growers] should be given to all visitors . . .' (*The Anatomy of Dessert*, 1933)

The number of available varieties is now much smaller than it was, but there are still a few nurseries which stock a good range. In fact, the 'brand leaders' Careless and Leveller are both good old sorts, well flavoured and recorded as far back as about 1850, but for ease of handling they are harvested commercially before they are fully grown and ripened. The best nurseries sell at least some of the four different colours of gooseberry: white, yellow, red and green. Still available (and selected for flavour) are:

Red: Dan's Mistake; Ironmonger; London (famous in shows); Whinham's Industry.

White: Whitesmith; Snowdrop; Hero of the Nile.

Yellow: Golden Drop; Broom Girl; Yellow Champagne; Golden Lion.

Green: Keepsake; Surprise; Alma.

(Suppliers: **Springhill**★ – send s.a.e. for their special list of 52 named varieties – **R. V. Roger Ltd**★ and **J. C. Allgrove Ltd**★)

Fruit refugia

Old hedgerows, woodland corners and commonland are increasingly vital sanctuaries for fruit varieties that are being rooted out of orchards.

The practice of planting (or simply conserving) fruit trees in wild situations almost certainly pre-dates orthodox fruit culture. Before formal orchards were established productive trees of crab, wild plum and cherry were no doubt left standing when woodland was cleared.

Later individual fruit trees inside woodlands were sometimes assigned to individual holdings. But the majority were regarded as common property – as were the cultivars that, by the early medieval period, were planted out on woodland edges and in hedgerows in many areas of northern Europe. These sites gave them a measure of protection, and meant that they did not get in the way of open field farming.

Surviving hedgerow fruit trees (chiefly apples, pears and plums) normally date from eighteenth or nineteenth-century smallholdings, when hedges were regarded as productive extensions of orchard and woodland.

Hedgerows and woodland can also be sites where new sports and seedlings appear. The Victoria plum was found in a wood in Sussex, and the double-fruiting raspberry Lloyd George in a wood near Corfe Castle.

The Whitty Pear

Planting out may have been the origin of the famous Whitty Pear in Wyre Forest, the only specimen of the sorb apple (or true service tree) *Sorbus domestica*, to have been found growing seemingly wild in Britain.

It was first recorded in 1678 and was already quite old. But it survived, to be burned down in 1862 by a poacher as an act of vengeance against a local magistrate who was particularly fond of the tree. Luckily grafts from the original tree had been grown on at nearby Arley Castle, and one of these was planted out at the ancestral site in Wyre Forest in 1913. Others were planted elsewhere in the vicinity of the Forest, and the superb specimen in the Oxford Botanic Gardens is reputed to have been grown from Wyre seed (though the fruits are rarely fertile in our climate).

The neglected windfall fruit in botanic gardens is your best chance of getting a taste of sorb apples. The tree is a member of the same family as the rowan (whitty pear is simply 'the rowan with pear-like fruit') but its fruits have more in common with its other relatives, the whitebeam and wild service tree. Like them its fruits need to be fully ripe and in the process of going soft ('bletting') before they are edible. They are pleasantly reminiscent of baked apples when raw, though on the Continent they're more commonly used for making jellies and fruit liqueurs.

Scrumping

Fruit from deliberately planted trees is, strictly speaking, private property, even if it appears to have gone wild or is overhanging a public path or highway. But no one is likely to object to windfall gathering or even a little small-scale scrumping. It helps spread the genes around, after all!

Please do remember, however, that the Theft Act of 1968 makes it illegal to collect even wild fruit for the sake of sale or reward. And in addition under the Criminal Damage Act 1971 it is illegal to deliberately damage a tree by, say, breaking off a whole branch instead of just the fruit.

Services rendered

The wild service, a relative of the whitebeam and rowan, is one of the most local and least known of all our native trees, and as a result we've lost touch with what is arguably the most delectable of all our wild fruits.

The story of the service's rise, decline and subsequent re-discovery is something of a parable of the changing fortunes of all our domestic plants. The fruits began as a neolithic tit-bit, gained enough popularity in some parts of England for houses, farms and pubs to be named after them, and then passed into obscurity as the tree's woodland habitat was destroyed and cheap exotic fruits became more easily available.

Over the past ten years Patrick Roper, a wild service enthusiast from the tree's heartland in the Weald, has revolutionized our view of its history and distribution. His research has shown that the tree occurs right across England and Wales, but is confined to hard limestone soils (in the west) and stiff clays. Spreading almost exclusively by suckers (seedlings are almost unknown in the wild), it is also restricted to long-established woodland, and to hedgerows derived from ancient woods.

The fruits, which are round or pear-shaped and the size of small cherries, are hard and bitter at first, but as the autumn progresses (and particularly with the first frosts) they 'blet' and turn soft, brown and very sweet. The taste is unlike anything else which grows wild in this country, with hints of tamarind, sultana, apricot and damson.

Remains of the berries have been found in a number of early archaeological sites, and they must have been a boon when other sources of sugar were in short supply. In areas where the tree was relatively widespread they continued to be a popular dessert fruit right up to the beginning of this century and grafted trees have been found in orchards. The fruits were gathered before they had bletted and strung up in clusters round a stick, which was hung up indoors, often by the hearth. They were picked off and eaten as they came, like sweets. In a good year the harvest could be enormous (one tree in the Weald with a 14-foot girth carries 2 tons of berries), and the surplus was either added to beer or fermented into a drink in its own right.

Patrick Roper suspects that a local name for the berries, Chequers, may derive from a pub which sold service-berry beer, and was then transferred to other pubs and buildings which had service trees nearby. The Chequers in Smarden, Kent, has a tree in its garden, and has inherited a recipe for bottling the berries (when hung up for bletting they are described as looking 'like a swarm of bees'). The drink, made by simply fermenting the berries with a little extra sugar, is strong and piquant, and ought to be revived in those areas where the trees still grow. As for those where they don't: in cultivation wild service will grow well from seed (though often not appearing till the second spring) and as well as bearing fruit, the trees have a visual bonus in their startling crimson leaves in autumn.

Wild Fruits

Blackberries

One of the most versatile and varied of all wild fruits. There are more than 400 micro-species in Britain, providing a huge range of variety in shape, size, fruiting time (the earliest are ripe in mid-August), sweetness and flavour. Blackberries can occur with distinct savours of grape, plum or even apple.

If any wild variety does take your fancy because of taste or particularly early or prolific fruiting, do try growing it on in your garden. Small cuttings will root easily, and seeds germinate sometimes even after the berries have been cooked! They should bear their first fruit in a couple of years.

Picking hints
With inconspicuous fruit – or shy fruiters – be methodical in your picking. Look inside the tree or bush. Work round it in both clockwise and anti-clockwise directions so that you have the light on different aspects of the branches. Use a walking stick to bend down branches gently. And gather the fruit into a basket that stays open whilst you're picking. There is a device on the market for this, consisting of a bag with a metal or wood-framed mouth, which clips over the wrist so that the bag hangs open, immediately under the free hand. It is expensive, but you can make your own with a carrier bag and a piece of wire.

Strawberries

Gilbert White mentions how after the felling of beech trees on Selborne Hanger masses of strawberries appeared on the 'slidder' – the wide, cleared track down which the trunks were slid to the bottom of the hill. Children gathered the fruit and took it to his door.

Wild strawberries growing in sunlit sites like this are especially delectable, because you can eat them warm. Best of all are those growing on limestone, warmed up by the heat reflected from the bare rock.

Try bordering paths and flowerbeds with wild and Alpine strawberries. They flower from June until September, grow in pretty clumps and produce delicious little fruits the

1 *Fragaria & Fraga.*
Red Strawberries.

2 *Fragaria & Fraga subalba.*
White Strawberries.

whole summer long. Several seed merchants sell seed of the wild strawberry and of the Alpine – usually Baron Solemacher. They are slow to germinate so don't give up too soon. They need to be planted out when two adult leaves have appeared.

Strange fruits

Cloudberry, *Rubus chamaemorus*. The sharp orange berries are very popular in Scandinavia, where they make a jelly to go with goat cheese. But for some reason cloudberry is a shy fruiter in this country where it is relatively widespread in the uplands. Apparently this has always been so. The fruits were so rare an occurrence in the Berwyn mountains that in the parish of Llanrhaiadr anyone bringing a quart of cloudberries to the parson on the morning of St Dogfan's (the parish saint) day would have his tithes remitted for the year.

Varieties of *Rubus chamaemorus* are sold in garden centres as ground cover plants, and these will often bear a sparse crop of fruit if planted in a sunny site.

Dewberry, *Rubus caesius*. Smaller than most blackberries, with fewer drupes and covered with a white grape-like bloom. When fully ripe it is so succulently juicy that it's impossible to pick without squashing. Use this fragility as an excuse for some decadent eating. Don't try and

Dewberry, Rubus caesius

pick the berry itself but snip off the whole shoot (with secateurs or large scissors) about one inch from the fruit. Serve the berries like this, complete with leaves for decoration and stalk for handling. Eat them one by one, like cocktail cherries, dipping them first in a bowl of cream and then in one of castor sugar.

Sea buckthorn, *Hippophae rhamnoides*. A silvery-leaved shrub that is often planted to stabilize coastal sand-dunes, where it can spread rampantly. Can be kept in better check in gardens. The bright orange berries make a jelly, rich in vitamin C (1200 mg per kg), that goes well with fish.

Sorrel, *Rumex acetosa*. Strictly a leaf vegetable, but its sour-grapeskin taste also qualifies it as a fruit. Florence White reported in her *Good Things in England* (1932) that

In Lancashire they still use the fresh young leaves of wild sorrel as a substitute for apple in turnovers. I have made it myself, and very good it is, with plenty of brown sugar and a little moisture on the leaves. Sorrel is in season between apples and gooseberries, i.e. April and May.

Directory

Books

Baker, Harry, 'Fruit' *RHS Encyclopaedia of Gardens* (Mitchell Beazley, 1980).

Greenoak, Francesca, *Forgotten Fruits* (Andre Deutsch, 1983).

Grigson, Jane, *Jane Grigson's Fruit Book* (Michael Joseph, 1982).

Harrison, S. G. *et al*, *The Oxford Book of Food Plants* (see *Vegetables*).

RHS, *The Fruit Garden Displayed* (1978).

Suppliers

J. C. Allgrove Ltd, The Nursery, Middle Green, Langley, Buckinghamshire, tel: 0753 20155.

Aylett's Nurseries, St Albans, Hertfordshire, tel: Bowmansgreen 22255.

Blackmoor Nurseries, Liss, Hampshire, tel: 042203 3576. Excellent fruit-tree nursery. Wholesale, but sells on a 'cash and carry' basis.

Deacons Nurseries, Godshill, Isle of Wight, tel: 098 389 750.

Family Trees, Summerlands, Curdbridge, Botley, Southampton, tel: 04892 6680.

Hillier Nurseries (Winchester) Ltd, Ampfield, Romsey, Hampshire, tel: 0794 68733. Excellent nurseries: very wide range of trees, fruit trees and roses.

New Tree Nurseries, 2 Nunnery Road, Canterbury, Kent, tel: 0227 61209.

R. V. Roger Ltd, The Nurseries, Pickering, North Yorkshire, tel: 0751 72226. Has six sorts of cobnuts, Alpine strawberries, Lancashire gooseberries and a good range of red currants.

St Bridget Nurseries, Old Rydon Lane, Exeter, tel: 039287 3672. Good all-round range.

Scotts Nurseries (Merriott) Ltd, Merriott, Somerset, tel: 0460 72306. Astonishing range of apples. Extremely informative catalogue.

Springhill Nurseries Ltd, Lang Stract, Aberdeen, tel: 0224 693788. Gooseberries.

Wyevale Nurseries, Kings Acre Road, Hereford, tel: 0432 65474.

Advisory services

Apple and Pear Development Council, Union House, The Pantiles, Tunbridge Wells, Kent, tel: 0892 20255 (Answerphone for names of fruit growers on fruit-tasting days: 0892 42872).

Fruit Identification Department, Royal Horticultural Society, Wisley, Ripley, Surrey, tel: 048643 3524.

Trees

Historically, trees were plants used and enjoyed in the wild. Available varieties were too big for most gardens and in any case there was an abundance of accessible trees in the farming landscape. The situation has now changed radically. 'Wild' trees are declining throughout the country, and increasingly gardeners are making use of more compact varieties to recreate some version of the vanishing wooded landscape in their own plots.

Below is a personal and very open-ended programme to help you choose trees for your own tastes and needs, inside the usual constraints of modern gardens:

A tree planner

1 Flowering trees: are you most moved by

  a) a golden cascade?

  b) 'loveliest of trees'?

  c) demure close-up beauty?

a) Laburnum – not simply a suburban tree; it looks surprisingly at home in a rural setting among farm buildings – and, planted thoughtfully, in a whole spectrum of different places.

b) Housman accurately described the cherry as 'hung with bloom along the bough'. The wild cherry, a most beautiful tree, is only for very large gardens, but some of the fruiting (sweet/amarello/acid) cherries are grafted on to less vigorous stocks and just recently the Colt stock breakthrough has meant that, while not dwarf, a smaller cherry tree has been made available for gardens (page 97).

Wild cherry, fruit (left)

Guelder rose

c) Guelder rose – one of the most beautiful small trees, perfect in every detail: a round head of flowers with its coronet of larger flowers; interestingly shaped and textured leaves; richly covered, carmine-coloured fruits.

2 'Each peach, pear, plum . . .' do you fancy

    a) a straightforward apple, pear, plum or cherry?

    b) a traditional tree which used to be planted in the alleys of old gardens for the benefit of its flowers and fruit?

    c) something really unusual to puzzle even the most knowing of your visitors?

a) Try an unstraightforward variety (it may be more trouble to find – but see Appendix – yet is no more difficult to grow).

b) Quince and medlars with their beautiful roselike flowers – the quince pale pink, the medlar heavy cream crepe – were planted in walks in medieval and sixteenth-century gardens as well as in orchards.

c) Consider the wild service (see page 103) with its sweet granular berries and crimson autumn foliage, or perhaps a named variety of walnut such as Franquette, or one of the cobnut varieties: Cosford Filbert or White Filbert.

3 Be adventurous with form as well as with species and variety. Do you have a good

    a) wall?

    b) a place where you would like to divide the garden lawn from vegetables or along a path?

    c) nowhere to do anything?

a) Try a fan-trained tree. You can buy them ready started or train it yourself – it's not difficult and much cheaper. Pears look well and often produce better fruit this way, and superb but recalcitrant plums like Coe's Golden Drop can be coaxed into fruit over the warm brick.

b) Try espaliers, these are decorative and fruitful – apples and pears are the traditional species. (See also page 95, also 92–3.)

c) Don't despair; fill a container with compost and grow a small-scale tree – if you've got a warm nook you could even try oranges and lemons.

But buy stock, don't raise it from seed if you want fruit. If you like the 'Chinese feet' version of trees you might try a Bonsai, but they need as much care as a pet.

4 *Déjeuner sous l'arbre* . . . a tree on the lawn is no trouble, so long as you make sure you have a sensible half-standard and not a dwarf form, and you can

   a) sit in its shade;
   b) augment your picnic from the branches;
   c) admire it from your windows.

a) Whitebeam thrives in the open, a pretty, flowerful and shapely tree, it is a delight throughout the year.

The Whitebeam, Pyrus aria

b & c) Find a fruit tree which also delights the eye. Ribston Pippin has beautiful foliage, rich, dark green above, felty-pale beneath; cherries see 1b above; Crab apples give blossom and fruit: variety John Downie has red late-summer apples which make excellent jelly.

5 Take time from the business of the day to enjoy the sensuous qualities of your trees, and plant them to indulge

   a) sight;
   b) your sense of smell;
   c) your ear.

a) Wander around parks and woods and discover what shapes and details most please you: the wide tall lattice of an ash, perhaps, the soft-edged handprint of field maple leaves; or the bunched needles and springtime 'roses' of the larch.

b) Who can resist the dizzy resinous scent of balsam poplar leaves in April (subgenus *Tacamahaca*: TT32 is a hybrid between *trichocarpa* and *balsamifera* and recommended by Alan Mitchell as a garden tree of erect growth). Poplars grow very fast but pollard happily.

c) Poplars again: the famed whisper of the aspen *Populus tremula* as the breeze catches its rounded wavy leaves on their long slender flattened stems.

6 Do you favour a species with special association with the place where you live: perhaps

  a) ecological?

  b) historical?

a) Tramp around your local parks and/or woodlands. You may find an ancient historical mulberry, or a sport tree whose form is not found elsewhere, or you may take to a tree which grows especially in your area like the native black poplar which appears unsung in many of Constable's paintings.

b) Consult a local historian or *Victoria County History* for famous boundary trees: hangman-oaks, cross oaks, wassailing apples and so on. County records, or helpful vicars with parish records may turn up an Anglo-Saxon charter with details of the tree species which marked parish boundaries.

Wild trees for the garden

These instructions for growing small native trees from seed are adapted from an excellent, no-nonsense guide prepared by the Devon Trust for Nature Conservation:

Seed sown in the autumn will not normally germinate until the following spring, or the one after. Therefore, it must be protected from mice and birds. Steeping means soaking the newly collected seed in water so that the fleshy outer fruit may more easily be removed. Stratifying is storing seed in moist sand or peat (to preserve it and to overcome dormancy) in mouse-proof boxes either buried in the ground or stored in an outhouse. If the latter, water occasionally as the seed must be kept moist. Collect seeds from healthy trees if possible.

Pollard ash

Silver birch

Field maple: Collect keys in October/November from trees if possible. Sow immediately or store dry over winter and stratify for six weeks before sowing in the first spring.

Blackthorn and hawthorn: Collect berries when ripe in autumn, stratify and sow in second spring.

Elder: Collect berries as soon as ripe, before the birds eat them, stratify and sow in second spring.

Hazel: Collect nuts as soon as husk browning begins and before squirrels become interested. Stratify and sow in the first spring following collection.

Holly: Collect berries late autumn or early spring. Dry before either storing or sowing. Autumn harvested seed may be sown in the autumn a year later or stratify until the following spring.

Rowan and bird cherry: Collect fruits as soon as ripe in August/September (before birds eat them). Partially dry, store in open container and sow in the first spring.

Birch: Collect catkins in late summer when seeds are still green enough to cluster together and spread out to dry for several weeks to prevent heating. Store over winter in sealed container and sow in first spring.

Alder: Cut small cone-bearing branches (complete with leaves) from the tree in autumn and hang up to dry. When leaves are dry shake branches to extract seed from cones and store in sealed containers and sow in first spring.

Guelder rose: Collect berries as soon as ripe (August/September). Stratify and sow in first spring.

Spindle: Collect berries when ripe (late summer/autumn), spread out in warm room for several days to dry, extract seed from fruit, then thoroughly dry the seed. Store in sealed container and sow in first spring.

Poplar or aspen: Collect catkins when the white down appears (April/May). Spread out under cover, and sheltered from winds. When the seed become fully exposed extract by placing uncleaned seed in a paper bag and blowing into it until the down and the seed separate, or rub through a fine sieve. Sow straight away.

Small-leaved lime: Collect seed when ripe (October), mainly from the ground and stratify for eighteen months. Sow in the second spring after collection.

Hornbeam: Collect seed September to November. Stratify for eighteen months. Sow in second spring after collection.

Sallows (Willows): Are best propagated by hard wood cuttings inserted in prepared beds in the open ground between November and February. The cuttings should be about 9″ long and planted firmly with no more than 3″ showing above ground.

(Acknowledgement is made to The Devon Trust for Nature Conservation.)

A phoenix from the elms

Despite Dutch elm disease, the British elm is far from extinct. Round the stumps of large numbers of dead and cleared trees (particularly the small-leaved and English elms) forests of suckers are appearing. They may not make it to full-sized trees, as the trunks can contract the fungus disease once they are about six or seven years old. But as a bonus we have a new shrub species in the landscape – and one of huge genetic variety. In East Anglia, for instance, Dr R. H. Richens has found that almost every village has its own unique variety of small-leaved elm, the result of centuries of suckering by favourite local trees and hedging from their cuttings. (See pp. 44–46, *The Common Ground*, Richard Mabey.★)

Woodland Rescue

The Woodland Trust★ is a major force for saving our vanishing native woodland. Since its formation in 1972 it has attracted more than 20,000 members, and purchased 80 woods totalling more than 2500 acres for public enjoyment. It has pioneered schemes for planting up new trees and woods in members' names – from one tree for as little as £1 to whole commemorative groves.

It is also running (at Pepper Wood, in the West Midlands) an experimental 'community woodland' managed by the local community under Trust guidance, and supplying produce for use locally as firewood, garden stakes, etc.

The Tree Council★ also encourages tree-planting schemes.

Lime tree

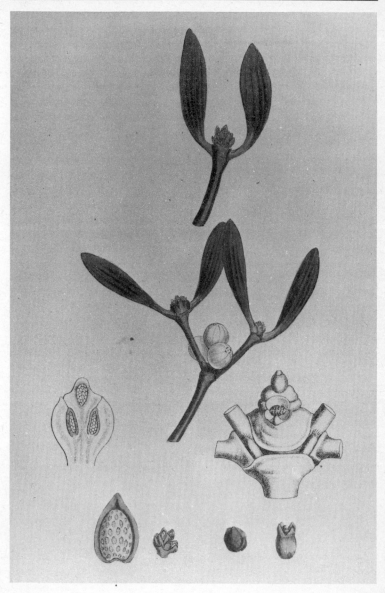

Mistletoe

Mistletoe

An agreeable parasite, whatever your view of its magical reputation, and a potential second crop from your fruit trees (or a first, if you grow soft-barked trees such as willow or poplar).

Here is one account of how to start a mistletoe clump from berries gathered in the wild:

It is essential to have a ripe berry. Mistletoe berries are fully ripe in February and March, and it will therefore be useless to try to perpetuate Christmas souvenirs. The method is simple, as is well known. Make a slight cut in the bark at a young joint. Do this on the under side, so that birds cannot get at the seed. Slightly raise the bark on each side of the cut, crush the berry [taken from a clump still on a tree] and gently push in the seed with some of the juicy flesh adhering. The bark should be firmly pressed down again to close the cut, and must be covered with gauze or muslin. Germination is slow, and, during the first year, only two small leaves will sprout. Once the growth is established the plant becomes hardy and will withstand any climate.

EDW, *The Countryman Gardening Book*, David and Charles, 1973

Witches brooms

Growths of bunched twigs, caused when viruses, bacteria or insects stimulate a whole cluster of dormant buds to grow out together on a branch. The change brought about by the attacking organism is genetic, and if twigs from a witches broom are planted out as cuttings, or grafted on

to normal rootstocks, freak trees result.

Spotted: a witches broom in a hazel bush in Wales carrying a perfectly formed dwarf nut, which had unfortunately vanished by the time it was ripe. Would it have germinated into another dwarf nut bush, given the chance?

Cuttings

If taking cuttings from wild trees, remember that the law prohibits the taking of more than small young shoots (see page 103) and that local by-laws (on nature reserves, for instance) may prohibit the taking of *any* plant material.

If you have some distance to travel with cuttings before potting them up, put them in *sealed* polythene bags, together with some moist newspaper or leaf mould.

Woodland management in the shrubbery

If you have trees, wild or planted, that are beginning to look too big for your garden, or are seeding too aggressively, try management as an alternative to uprooting or felling. Ashes, sycamore, all types of willow and poplar, even eucalyptus, will respond well to regular *pollarding* (lopping top branches to about 5 to 10 feet above ground) and *coppicing* (cutting the tree back to ground level every few years).

- Ash (known in various counties as —shire weed) will regenerate with a number of separate stems even when cut back in its first year, and in a garden with plenty of light makes a shapely, feathery bush. When it grows too large for your comfort, simply repeat the procedure, and use the poles in the garden as stakes or bean sticks.

- Sycamore, which can be a troublesomely prolific seeder when mature, can be treated in the same way, and cut back to ground level as often as every three or four years, providing abundant poles for firewood or garden work (and, incidentally, preventing seeding).

- Established willows can be safely cut back every year, and in the case of the coloured bark varieties (e.g. the red Vittelina) this is a way of producing dense layers of winter colour in shrub beds.

Tree Protection Orders

The chief legal protection for trees of landscape or historic importance is the Tree Preservation Order (TPO) which in theory can be made by a local planning authority whenever the felling or lopping of a tree, group of trees or woodland would injure a neighbourhood's amenity. In practice some authorities are notably less keen on them than others.

Any individual or society can press their local planning authority to impose a TPO, but they should remember the following considerations:

a) *Single* trees are normally considered only if they are of great historic or landscape importance.

b) The trees must be healthy.

c) TPOs are not usually thought to be appropriate to trees on private land where there has been woodland husbandry of a high standard. Village green trees, boundary hedgerows, pondside willows – these are ideal subjects.

Do continue to lobby your planning authority if you and your neighbours care about a particular tree, and be vigilant. If you are in doubt about whether a TPO does (or should) apply to a particular tree, and you suspect it is about to be felled, contact your local planning office immediately.

And since time is of the essence, be prepared to take direct action in the form of occupying or surrounding the tree. The fines for defying TPOs are paltry (£400 or twice the timber value of the tree, whichever is greater) and no real deterrent to a developer. Physically preventing illicit felling can mean that a local planning authority can have time to talk to the prospective feller, and perhaps obtain the more formidable legal obstacle of an injunction against felling.

For further details, see *Tree Preservation Orders*, Advisory leaflet No. 1, from the **Arboricultural Association.***

A celebrity tree, 'The Maple of Ratibor'
the famous three-storey tree-house of the Piedmont: a place for people
to meet, a landmark and a curiosity

Directory

Books

Beckett, Gillian and Kenneth, *Planting Native Trees and Shrubs* (Jarrold, 1979).

Johnson, Hugh, *The International Book of Trees* (Mitchell Beazley, 1973).

Mabey, Richard, *The Common Ground* (Hutchinson, 1980).

Mitchell, Alan, *The Gardener's Book of Trees* (Dent, 1981).

Mitchell, Alan, *The Trees of Britain and Northern Europe* (Collins, 1982).

Rackham, Oliver, *Trees and Woodland in the British Landscape* (Dent, 1976).

Suppliers

Goscote Nurseries Ltd, Syston Road, Cossington, Leicester.

Hillier Nurseries, Winchester, Hampshire, tel: 0794 68733.

Lound Manor, Lound, Lowestoft, Suffolk.

Notcutts Nurseries Ltd, Woodbridge, Suffolk.

Ben Reid & Co. Ltd, Pinewood Park, Counteswells Road, Aberdeen.

R. V. Roger Ltd (see *Fruit*)

Romney Marsh Garden Centre, Ham Street, Ashford, Kent.

Scotts Nurseries Ltd, Merriott, Somerset, tel. 0751 72226.

Sunningdale Nurseries Ltd, London Road, Windlesham, Surrey.

Wyevale Nurseries, Kings Acre Road, Hereford, tel: Hereford 65474.

Societies

Arboricultural Association, 52 Hilliard Road, Northwood, Middlesex.

Tree Council, 35 Belgrave Square, London SW1.

Woodland Trust, Westgate, Grantham, Lincolnshire.

Appendix
Gardens Open to the Public

Berkshire

The Old Vicarage, Bucklebury W I
Education Centre, Denham College,
Nr Abingdon (herb garden)

Buckinghamshire

Ascott Gardens, Wing (topiary
sundial).

Milton's Cottage, Chalfont St Giles
(John Milton's cottage, cottage
garden, roses, flowering shrubs,
fruit trees).

Chenies Manor, Chenies (herb
garden).

Cambridgeshire

The Botanic Garden, Cambridge
(herb garden).

Emmanuel College, Cambridge
(herb garden).

Cheshire

Arley Hall and Gardens, Northwich
(very early twin herbaceous borders,
shrub roses).

Little Moreton Hall, Congleton
(traditional knot and herb gardens).

Cornwall

Bearoak Gardens, Michaelstow, St
Tudy (garden of plants useful to
man; over 350 varieties; large herb
garden).

County Demonstration Garden,
Probus, Nr St Austell (display plots
showing every aspect of cultivation).

Cumbria

Acorn Bank, Temple Sowerby (herb
and walled gardens; fruit trees and
wild garden).

Levens Hall, Nr Kendal
(Elizabethan house with topiary
garden laid out in 1692).

Derbyshire

Haddon Hall, Bakewell (medieval
and manorial home; terraces and
wall and bed roses).

Hardwick Hall, Chesterfield (herb
garden; orchards and a collection of
old-fashioned roses).

Devon

Castle Drogo, Drewsteignton (herb
garden).

Dartington Hall and Gardens, Nr
Totnes (terraced garden dating back
to medieval times).

The Old Barn, Fremington (herb
garden).

Rosemoor Garden Trust, Great
Torrington (species and
old-fashioned roses).

Tapley Park, Instow, Nr Bideford, N. Devon (walled kitchen garden).

Dorset

Athelhampton, Nr Puddletown (six walled gardens, architectural yews, rare plants, dovecote).

Highbury, Nr Wimborne (herb garden).

Essex

Beth Chatto Gardens, Nr Colchester (a 'gardener's garden', set in a hollow, with many unusual plants both for dry and damp gardens).

St Osyth's Priory, Clacton-on-Sea (rose garden and fine topiary).

Gloucestershire

Barnsley House Garden, Barnsley, Cirencester (established garden with eighteenth-century summerhouses, herbaceous plants, laburnum walk, knot and herb gardens; kitchen garden laid out as decorative *potager*).

Dower House, Badminton (herb garden).

Hidcote Manor Gardens, Mickleton (seventeenth-century Cotswold house with one of the most beautiful English gardens; herb garden).

Kiftsgate Court, Nr Chipping Campden (unusual shrubs and plants).

Sudeley Castle, Winchcombe, Cheltenham (historic Elizabethan gardens).

Westbury Court, Westbury-on-Sea (herb garden).

Hampshire

Beaulieu, Nr Lyndhurst (abbey ruins with medieval herb garden).

Holywell, Swanmore (herb garden).

Longstock Park Gardens, Stockbridge (herb garden).

Mechelmersh Court, Romsey (herb garden).

Mottisfont Abbey, Mottisfont (collection of old-fashioned roses).

Spinners, Lymington (primulas, blue poppies and other woodland and ground cover plants).

Sutton Manor Herb Farm, Sutton Manor, Sutton Scotney, Winchester (herb garden).

West Green House, Hartley Wintney (herb garden).

Hereford

Abbey Dore Court, Hereford (herb garden).

Hergest Croft Gardens, Kington (old-fashioned vegetable garden).

Hertfordshire

Capel Manor Institute of Horticulture, Waltham Cross (herb garden).

Hatfield House, Hatfield (herb garden).

Kent

Eyehorne Manor, Hollingbourne (herb garden).

Hall Place Gardens, Bexley (medieval/Jacobean mansion; herb and peat gardens; topiary 'Queen's Beasts'; conservatory).

Hever Castle, Nr Edenbridge (herb garden).

Knole, Sevenoaks (herb garden).

Penshurst Place, Penshurst (ten-acre walled garden with hedged enclosures – a Tudor legacy).

The Salutation, Sandwich (restored five-acre garden based on designs of Lutyens and Jekyll).

Scotney Castle, Nr Lamberhurst (herb garden).

Sissinghurst Castle, Nr Cranbrook (herb garden).

Withersdane Hall, Nr Ashford (herb garden).

Lancashire

Hoghton Tower, Nr Preston (sixteenth-century hilltop mansion; three walled gardens).

Leicestershire

Stone Cottage, Hambleton (herb garden).

Lincolnshire

Gunby Hall, Burgh-le-Marsh (herb garden).

London

Chelsea Physic Garden (herb garden, special request only).

Fulham Palace Gardens (herb garden).

Greenwich Park (herbs in borders).

The Herb Garden, The Queen's House, Kew Gardens (herb garden).

Queen Mary's Rose Garden, Regent's Park (roses).

Norfolk

Felbrigg Hall, Houghton (herb garden).

Mannington Hall Gardens, Saxthorpe (rose garden, scented garden, chapel garden, walled garden).

Northamptonshire

Delapré Gardens, Northampton (walled garden dating back to fifteenth century; garden and walls laid out as Victorian garden; herbs and herbaceous borders; shrubs, arboretum).

Rockingham Castle, Corby (ancient home set in wild and formal gardens; rose garden and 'elephant' hedge).

Northumberland

Lindisfarne Castle walled garden (sixteenth-century castle, restored by Lutyens in 1900, garden designed by Gertrude Jekyll and restored by the National Trust).

Seaton Delaval Hall, Seaton Sluice, Whitley Bay (eighteenth-century box parterre and statuary; rose garden).

Nottinghamshire

South Collingham House, Collingham (herb garden).

Oxfordshire

Bampton Manor, Bampton (herb garden).

Greys Court, Nr Henley-on-Thames (gardens surrounded by ancient walls).

Manor Farm Museum, Cogges, Witney (farm dating from the medieval period; walled kitchen garden and orchard being restored to its Edwardian appearance).

Marndhill, Ardington (herb garden).

John Mattock Rose Nurseries, Nuneham Courtenay (over 300,000 roses grown annually from leading rose hybridists of the world, including some old varieties).

Troy, Ewelme (herb garden).

Shropshire

Mawley Hall, Cleobury Mortimer (herb garden).

Oak Cottage Herb Farm, Nesscliff (herb garden).

Somerset

The American Museum, Nr Bath (herb garden).

Barrington Court, Ilminster (walled gardens with lilies, roses and iris).

East Lambrook Manor, South Petherton (herb garden).

Gaulden Manor, Tolland (herb garden).

Orchard House, Claverton (herb garden).

Staffordshire

The Bradshaws, Wrottesley (herb garden).

Moseley Old Hall, Wolverhampton (herb garden).

Suffolk

Gainsborough's House, Sudbury (herb garden).

Ixworth Priory, Nr Bury St Edmunds (herb garden).

Lime Kiln, Claydon (old roses)

Thornham Herbs, the Walled Garden, Thornham Magna, Nr Eye (herb garden).

Surrey

Canbury Gardens, Kingston-on-Thames (fragrance gardens for the blind).

Hampton Court Palace and Gardens, East Molesey (Henry VIII's gardens and parkland; Tudor knot garden, maze and grape vine).

Sussex

Batemans, Burwash (herb garden).

Coke's Cottage, West Burton (herb garden).

Gravetye Manor, East Grinstead (herb garden).

Great Dixter, Northiam, East Sussex (sunken garden with lily pond and flowering meadows).

Warwickshire

Anne Hathaway's Cottage, Stratford-upon-Avon (herb garden).

Queen's Park, Harborne, Birmingham (fragrance garden for the blind).

Shakespeare Gardens, Stratford-upon-Avon (New Place gardens with knot garden and ancient mulberry tree).

Worcestershire

Snowshill Manor, Broadway (Tudor house set in small, formal terraced garden).

Wiltshire

The Courts, Holt (topiary, arboretum, lily pond).

Hillbarn House, Great Bedwin (herb garden).

Lackham College of Agriculture, Lacock (herb garden).

Sheldon Manor, Chippenham (old-fashioned roses, water garden, ancient yew trees, rare plants).

Yorkshire

Castle Howard, York (rose gardens).

York Gate, Adel, Leeds (herb garden).

Wales

Bible Garden, Bangor (herb garden).

St Fagan's Garden, Cardiff (herb garden).

For further details (opening times, facilities, etc.) consult the following booklets available from most bookshops:

English Herb Gardens and Farms to Visit, available from Mr H. E. Bates, The British Herb Trade Association, Middleton Tyas, Richmond, Yorkshire.

Garden Britain Observer Map, available from Edward Stanford Ltd, 12–14 Long Acre, London WC2.

Gardens of England and Wales Open to the Public, available from the National Garden Scheme, 57 Lower Belgrave Street, London SW1.

Gardens to Visit, available from Gardener's Sunday Organisation.

National Trust Guides, details of membership from 42 Queen Anne's Gate, London SW1.

Scotland's Gardens, available from Scotland's Gardens Scheme, 26 Castle Terrace, Edinburgh.

Visit an English Garden, available from The English Tourist Board, 4 Grosvenor Gardens, London SW1.

ARENA

'Much more than a climbing book ... as much an adventure of romantic discovery as one of physical challenge'

CHRIS BONINGTON

SACRED SUMMITS
Peter Boardman

'In the east a distant spire rose from a crown of rock. The Matterhorn. Little more than a century ago, the natives of its surrounding valleys felt an invisible cordon drawn around it. To them the mountains were to be feared and suspected as haunts of monsters, wizards and crabbed goblins – and the devil. The mountains, trees, rocks and springs of Europe were respected then as sacred places. Man had felt his links with them, but then had broken with this heritage and had buried this delicate magic of life. I knew the mountain, earth set upon earth, would remain silent long after I had stopped...'

SACRED SUMMITS

This is the story of a year in the life of a climber: three expeditions, each very different from one another in mood and style, to sacred mountains around the world. Tragically, the last book that the brilliant young mountaineer Peter Boardman was to write, *Sacred Summits* is a dramatic and moving testament to one man's will not to conquer but to understand.

'Poignant, vivid ... he gets closer to the strange mystique of mountaineering than many more pretentious writers'   *Observer*

WORDS
Paul Dickson

A connoisseur's collection of old and new, weird and wonderful, useful and outlandish words.

While others are content to collect coins, stock certificates, or butterflies, Paul Dickson collects words. Funny words, obscure words, new words, old words, sexy words, insulting words – even words we forgot we had.

Included in this remarkable collection are:

*A fresh and vibrant set of expletives that begs to be used in place of the tired group we have now (see, for example, 'amplexus' and 'culch').

*The rules for proper Pig Latin, Double Dutch, Opish and other secret languages.

*A major examination of the subtle differences among the indefinite nouns chingus, doodah, framus, gilhoolie, ipses, oojah and windge.

WORDS

The last word for word lovers everywhere.

'A marvellous book ... breathtaking' *Spectator*

APRIL ASHLEY'S ODYSSEY
Duncan Fallowell and April Ashley

George Jamieson was raised as a boy, but he never became a man. Instead he became Toni April, cabaret artiste, then April Ashley, a transsexual of nationwide renown and later, if briefly, Mrs Arthur Corbett, daughter-in-law of Lord Rowallan and an international personality. How did a boy from a Liverpool slum come to crash the barriers of both sex and class to become one of the most talked-about, controversial and unforgettable personalities of our times?

A daring, disturbing and shocking journey from the safety and protection of conventional society into the precariously balanced world of the transsexual – the most candid story of its kind.

'A camp *Tristram Shandy* that captures all the vitality of its subject's personality' *Tatler*

'It has more wisdom than a bench-load of judges and more wit than a crate of comics . . . her courage and honesty are devastating' *Spectator*

'Vivid ... serious'
New Standard